CW00833598

Easy Italian Phrase Book

1,600+ Common Phrases and Vocabulary for Beginners and Travelers in Italy

Also available:

Italian Short Stories for Beginners (https://geni.us/italianshorts)

Italian Grammar for Beginners (https://geni.us/italiangrammar1)

Table of Contents

Introduction

You probably picked up this phrasebook for one of these reasons: a) you're starting to learn Italian and want to have a bit of a head start by learning Italian phrases, or b) you're planning to travel to Italy soon.

Whether your reason is A or B, or both, that's wonderful news. Learning Italian phrases can open so many doors for you in both instances—literally and otherwise.

Some would say that learning Italian is not a necessity when you're traveling to Italy. Yes, in fact it isn't a requirement. If you stick to the major cities, you can get by without speaking a word of Italian. But being able to speak some basic phrases will make a world of difference to your travel experience.

If you wish to have as authentic an experience as possible, learning even a few basic phrases will help greatly.

If you want to be more than just a tourist and more of a real traveler, you need to know the most useful phrases.

You'll see the difference in how the shopkeeper, bartender, and locals will brighten up and exude more warmth at hearing you extend the courtesy of speaking to them in their language. You will have a more positive experience in your travels—that's guaranteed.

That's the aim of this book

This book wants to make your traveling experience in Italy as smooth as possible by giving you all the phrases and vocabulary you need to communicate in Italian in a simple way.

This is not a book that will teach you the entirety of the Italian language. But it is a great guide to help you navigate all kinds of scenarios during your travels in Italy: from arriving at the airport, getting around, and doing touristy activities, to the more serious situations such as facing untoward events and emergencies.

This is a book that will make you feel confident when facing any kind of scenario during your travels. Plus, it has bonus materials that will equip you with what you need to make the most of your vacation.

Here's what you'll find inside:

- **1,600+ Italian words and expressions with English translations.** It includes an easy phonetic pronunciation guide.
- **Audio** to help you practice your listening and pronunciation skills in Italian.
- **A menu reader to help you order the right food.** It contains food vocabulary and Italian dishes translated from Italian to English.
- **A pronunciation guide.** Each phrase comes with a simple phonetic script to help you quickly pronounce it like native speakers do.

Aside from tourists, this book will also benefit those who wish to give a boost to their Italian language lessons. If you are a beginner level learner or you have previously studied Italian but would like to review some basic phrases, this book is also great for you.

I hope you'll enjoy this book.

Grazie.

The Talk in Italian Team

Important! The link to download the audio files is available at the end of this book. (Page 171)

Part 1 – Essentials / I fondamentali

Chapter 1: The Italian basics / Le frasi di base

This chapter will be the most useful when you need help getting out of a difficult situation.

__Listen to track 1__

Italian	Pronunciation	English
Salve. / Ciao. (inf)	*[sal-vey / cha-oh]*	Hello. / Hi.
Arrivederci. / Ciao.	*[ah-ree-veh-der-chi / cha-oh]*	Goodbye. / Bye.
Scusi, signore/ signora!	*[scoo-see, see-nyoh-reh/see-nyoh-rah]*	Excuse me! (to catch attention)
Mi spiace!	*[mee spee-a-che]*	Sorry!
Mi scusi.	*[mee scoo-see]*	Excuse me.
Mi dispiace.	*[mee dees-pyah-cheh]*	I am sorry.
Grazie (mille).	*[grah-tzyeh (meel-leh)]*	Thanks (very much).
Per favore.	*[pehr fah-voh-reh]*	Please.
Lei parla inglese?	*[leh-ee pahr-lah een-gleh-seh]*	Do you speak English?
Qualcuno qui parla inglese?	*[qwahl-coo-noh qwee pahr-lah een-gleh-seh]*	Does anyone here speak English?

| Io parlo solo inglese. | *[ee-oh pahr-loh soh-loh een-gleh-seh]* | I speak only English. |
| Io parlo un po' l'italiano. | *[ee-oh pahr-loh oon poh ee-tah-lyah-noh]* | I speak a little Italian. |

Listen to track 2

La prego, parli più lentamente.	*[lah preh-goh, pahr-lee pyoo lehn-tah-mehn-teh]*	Please speak more slowly.
Io (non) capisco.	*[ee-oh (nohn) cah-pees-coh]*	I (do not) understand.
Mi capisce?	*[mee cah-pee-sheh]*	Do you understand me?
Può ripetere, per favore?	*[pwoh ree-peh-teh-reh, pehr fah-voh-reh]*	Could you repeat it, please?
Lo scriva, per favore.	*[loh scree-vah, pehr fah-voh-reh]*	Write it down, please.
Cosa significa questo?	*[coh-sah see-nyee-fee-cah qwes-toh]*	What does this mean?
Prego. / Di nulla.	*[preh-goh / dee nul-lah]*	You are welcome.
Come si dice "xx" in Italiano?	*[coh-meh see dee-cheh "xx" een ee-tah-lyah-noh]*	How do you say "xx" in Italian?
Come si scrive "xx"?	*[coh-meh see scree-veh "xx"]*	How do you write "xx"?

Può farmi lo spelling di "xx"?	*[pwoh fahr-mee loh spehl-leeng dee "xx"]*	Can you spell "xx"?
Cos'è quello?	*[coh-seh qwel-loh]*	What is that?
No.	*[noh]*	No.
Forse.	*[fohr-seh]*	Perhaps.
Sì.	*[see]*	Yes.

Listen to track 3

Sono un cittadino degli Stati Uniti d'America.	*[soh-noh oon chee-tah-dee-noh deh-lee stah-tee oo-nee-tee dah-meh-ree-cah]*	I am a United States citizen.
Il mio indirizzo è XX.	*[eel mee-oh een-dee-reet-zoh eh XX]*	My address is XX.
Cosa desidera?	[coh-zah deh-see-deh-rah]	What do you want?
Venga qui. / Vieni qui. (inf)	*[vehn-gah qwee / vee-eh-nee qwee]*	Come here.
Entri. / Entrate. (pl)	*[ehn-tree / ehn-trah-teh]*	Come in.
Attenda un momento. / Aspetti un attimo.	*[att-tehn-dah oon moh-mehn-toh / ah-speh-tee oon ah-tee-moh]*	Wait a moment.
Vado di fretta.	*[vah-doh dee fret-tah]*	I am in a hurry.

Ho caldo/ freddo.	*[hoh cahl-do/ freh-doh]*	I am warm/cold.
Ho fame/sete.	*[hoh fah-meh/ seh-teh]*	I am hungry/ thirsty.
Sono occupato/ stanco.	*[soh-noh oh-coo-pah-toh/ stahn-coh]*	I am busy/tired.
Mi fa piacere. / Sono lieto.	*[mee fah pya-cheh-reh / soh-noh lee-eh-toh]*	I am glad.
Che c'è? / Che succede, qui?	*[keh cheh / keh sooh-cheh-deh qwee]*	What is the matter here?
Va tutto bene.	*[vah tooh-toh beh-neh]*	It is all right.

Listen to track 4

Io (non) lo so.	*[ee-oh (nohn) loh soh]*	I (do not) know.
Io (non) credo.	*[ee-oh (nohn) creh-doh]*	I (do not) think so.
Non fa niente. / Non importa.	*[nohn fah nee-ehn-teh / nohn eem-pohr-tah]*	It doesn't matter.
Quant'è?	*[qwan-teh]*	How much is it?
È tutto!	*[eh toot-toh]*	That is all.
Può aiutarmi/ dirmi?	*[pwoh ah-yoo-tahr-mee/deer-mee]*	Can you help me/ tell me?
Dov'è il bagno?	*[doh-veh eel bah-nyoh]*	Where is the washroom?

il bagno degli uomini	*[eel bah-nyoh deh-lee wo-mee-nee]*	the men's room
il bagno delle donne	*[eel bah-nyoh deh-leh don-neh]*	the ladies room
Sto cercando il mio albergo/hotel.	*[stoh cher-cahn-doh eel mee-oh ahl-behr-goh/hotel]*	I am looking for my hotel.
Vorrei andarci a piedi.	*[voh-reh-ee ahn-dahr-chee ah pee-eh-dee]*	I would like to walk there.

Listen to track 5

Perché?	*[pehr-keh]*	Why?
Quando?	*[qwan-doh]*	When?
Chi?	*[kee]*	Who?
Cosa?	*[coh-sah]*	What?
Come?	*[coh-meh]*	How?
Quanto tempo?	*[qwahn-toh tem-poh]*	How long?
Quanto dista?	*[qwahn-toh dees-tah]*	How far?
qui	*[qwee]*	here
lì/là	*[lee / lah]*	there
a	*[ah]*	to
da	*[dah]*	from
con	*[kohn]*	with
senza	*[sehn-zah]*	without

Listen to track 6

dentro/in/nel (m)/nella (f)/ nello (m)	*[dehn-troh/ een/nehl/neh- lah/neh-loh]*	in
sopra	*[soh-prah]*	on
vicino	*[vee-chee-noh]*	near
lontano	*[lohn-tah-noh]*	far
davanti	*[dah-vahn-tee]*	in front of
dietro	*[dee-eh-troh]*	behind
accanto	*[ah-kahn-toh]*	beside
all'interno	*[ahl-een-tehr- noh]*	inside
all'esterno	*[ahl-ehs-tehr- noh]*	outside
vuoto	*[voo-oh-toh]*	empty
pieno	*[pee-eh-noh]*	full
qualcosa	*[qwal-coh-sah]*	something
niente	*[nee-ehn-teh]*	nothing
parecchio	*[pah-reh- kyoh]*	several

Listen to track 7

poco	*[poh-coh]*	few
(molto) di più	*[(mohl-toh) dee pyoo]*	(much) more
meno	*[meh-noh]*	less
(poco) di più	*[(poh-coh) dee pyoo]*	(a little) more
basta	*[bah-stah]*	enough
troppo	*[troh-poh]*	too much
tanto	*[tahn-toh]*	many

buono/bene	*[bwoh-noh/ beh-neh]*	good
più buono (di)/ migliore (di)	*[pyoo bwoh-noh (dee)/mee-lyoh-reh (dee)]*	better (than)
il migliore	*[eel mee-lyoh-reh]*	the best
cattivo	*[cah-tee-voh]*	bad
peggio (di)/ peggiore (di)	*[peh-djoh (dee)/peh-djoh-reh (dee)]*	worse (than)

Listen to track 8

adesso	*[ah-deh-soh]*	now
subito	*[soo-bee-toh]*	immediately
presto	*[preh-stoh]*	soon
più tardi	*[pyoo tahr-dee]*	later
il prima possibile	*[eel pree-mah poh-see-bee-leh]*	as soon as possible
È (troppo) tardi.	*[eh (troh-poh) tahr-dee]*	It is (too) late.
È presto.	*[eh preh-stoh]*	It is early.
lentamente	*[lehn-tah-mehn-teh]*	slowly
più lentamente	*[pyoo lehn-tah-mehn-teh]*	slower
velocemente	*[veh-loh-cheh-mehn-teh]*	quickly
più veloce	*[pyoo veh-loh-cheh]*	faster

Listen to track 9

Attenzione!	*[ah-tehn-zyoh-neh]*	Look out!
ascolti/ascolta (inf)	*[ah-scohl-tee/ ah-scohl-tah]*	listen
Guardi qui. / Guarda qui. (inf)	*[gwahr-dee qwee / gwahr-dah qwee]*	Look here.
Comprende? / Capisci? (inf)	*[com-prehn-deh / cah-pee-shee]*	Do you understand?
Cosa significa (XX)?	*[coh-sah see-nee-fee-cah (XX)]*	What does (XX) mean?
Come...?	*[coh-meh]*	How do you...?
...si pronuncia questo	*[see proh-noon-cha qwes-toh]*	...pronounce this
...si scrive (Buongiorno)	*[see scree-veh (bwon-johr-noh)]*	...write (Buongiorno)

Chapter 2: Difficulties / Le difficoltà

Listen to track 10

Non riesco a trovare l'indirizzo del mio albergo.	*[nohn ree-eh-scoh ah troh-vah-reh leen-dee-reet-zoh dehl mee-oh ahl-behr-goh]*	I cannot find my hotel address.
Ho perso i miei amici.	*[oh pehr-soh ee mee-eh-ee ah-mee-chee]*	I have lost my friends.
Ho lasciato il mio portafoglio in albergo.	*[oh lah-shah-toh eel myoh pohr-tah-foh-lyo een ahl-behr-goh]*	I left my purse/ wallet in the hotel.
Ho dimenticato i soldi/le chiavi.	*[oh dee-mehn-tee-cah-toh ee sohl-dee/leh kyah-vee]*	I forgot my money/keys.
Ho perso il mio treno.	*[oh pehr-soh eel myoh treh-noh]*	I have missed my train.
Cosa devo fare?	*[coh-sah deh-voh fah-reh]*	What should I do?
I miei occhiali sono rotti.	*[ee mee-eh-ee oh-kyah-lee soh-noh roh-tee]*	My glasses are broken.

Dove posso farli riparare?	*[doh-ve poh-soh fahr-lee ree-pah-rah-reh]*	Where can they be repaired?
un apparecchio acustico	*[oon ah-pah-reh-kyoh ah-coo-stee-coh]*	a hearing aid
ufficio oggetti smarriti	*[oof-fee-choh oh-djet-tee smah-ree-tee]*	the lost and found desk
il consolato Americano	*[eel cohn-soh-lah-toh ah-meh-ree-cah-noh]*	the American consulate
l'ambasciata Americana	*[lahm-bah-shah-tah ah-me-ree-cah-nah]*	the American embassy
il commissariato di polizia	*[eel com-miss-sah-ryah-toh dee poh-lee-zee-ah]*	the police station
Chiamerò un poliziotto.	*[kyah-meh-roh oon poh-lee-zyoh-toh]*	I will call a policeman.
Sono stato derubato.	*[soh-noh stah-toh deh-roo-bah-toh]*	I've been robbed.

Listen to track 11

Ho perso...	*[oh pehr-soh]*	I've lost...
Mi hanno rubato...	*[mee ah-noh roo-bah-toh]*	...was/were stolen.

...il mio zaino	*[eel mee-oh zah-ee-noh]*	...my backpack
...le mie valigie	*[leh mee-eh vah-lee-djeh]*	...my bags
...la mia carta di credito	*[lah mee-ah cahr-tah dee creh-dee-toh]*	...my credit card
...la mia borsa	*[lah mee-ah bohr-sah]*	...my handbag
...i miei gioielli	*[ee mee-eh-ee jo-yell-lee]*	...my jewelry
...i miei soldi	*[ee mee-eh-ee sohl-dee]*	...my money
...il mio passaporto	*[eel mee-oh pahs-sah-pohr-toh]*	...my passport
...i miei traveller cheque	*[ee mee-eh-ee trah-veh-lehr che-k]*	...my traveler's checks
...il mio portafoglio	*[eel mee-oh pohr-tah-foh-lyoh]*	...my wallet
Vorrei contattare...	*[voh-reh-ee cohn-tah-tah-reh]*	I want to contact...
...il mio consolato	*[eel mee-oh cohn-soh-lah-toh]*	...my consulate
...la mia ambasciata	*[lah mee-ah ahm-bah-shah-tah]*	...my embassy

Part 2: Greetings, introduction, social conversation / Saluti, introduzione e conversazione

Chapter 3: Social interactions / Interazione sociale

The main point of speaking Italian is to use the language in everyday conversation. As intimidating as it can be to converse in a different language, this is the ultimate goal of your studies. It is a good idea to have some basic phrases up your sleeve for when you are having conversations with people in Italian. These handy conversation starters and tips are ideal for those times when you need something relevant to say to keep the dialogue going.

Listen to track 12

Per favore.	*[pehr fah-voh-reh]*	Please.
Grazie (mille).	*[grah-tsyeh (meel-leh)]*	Thanks (very much).
Prego!	*[preh-goh]*	You're welcome!
Sì, grazie.	*[see, grah-tsyeh]*	Yes, please.
No, grazie.	*[no, grah-tsyeh]*	No, thanks.
Ok! / Va bene.	*[oh-keh-ee / vah beh-neh]*	OK!
Signor/Sig.	*[see-nyor]*	Sir/Mr.
Signora/Sig.ra	*[see-nyoh-rah]*	Madam/Mrs./Ms.
Signorina/Sig.na	*[see-nyoh-ree-nah]*	Miss
Salve. / Ciao	*[sahl-veh / cha-oh]*	Hello. / Hi.
Arrivederci. / Ciao.	*[Ah-ree-veh-dehr-chee / cha-oh]*	Goodbye. / Bye.
Ci vediamo.	*[chee veh-dyah-moh]*	Bye for now.

Listen to track 13

Buon giorno.	*[bwon djohr-noh]*	Good morning.
Buona sera.	*[bwoh-nah seh-rah]*	Good evening.
Buona notte.	*[bwoh-nah not-teh]*	Good night.
A domani.	*[ah doh-mah-nee]*	See you tomorrow.
Mi scusi!	*[mee scoo-see]*	Excuse me! (to catch attention)
Mi scusi! / Chiedo scusa!	*[mee scoo-see / kee-eh-doh scoo-sah]*	Sorry!
Mi dispiace.	*[mee dees-pyah-cheh]*	I'm sorry.
Come va?	*[coh-meh vah]*	How are you?
Bene, grazie.	*[beh-neh, grah-tsyeh]*	Fine, thanks.
E lei/tu (inf)?	*[eh leh-ee/too]*	And you?

Listen to track 14

Io non capisco.	*[ee-oh nohn cah-pees-coh]*	I don't understand.
Parlo molto poco l'italiano.	*[pahr-loh mohl-toh poh-coh lee-tah-lyah-noh]*	I speak very little Italian.
Grazie mille.	*[grah-tsyeh meel-leh]*	Thank you very much.
Come ti chiami?	*[coh-meh tee kyah-mee]*	What's your name?

Mi chiamo...	*[mee kyah-moh]*	My name is...
Piacere di conoscerti!	*[pyah-cheh-reh dee coh-noh-sher-tee]*	Pleased to meet you!
Piacere di conoscerla.	*[pyah-cheh-reh dee coh-noh-sher-lah]*	Delighted to meet you.
Questo/questa è mio marito/ mia moglie.	*[qwes-toh/ qwes-tah eh myoh mah-ree-toh/myah moh-lyeh]*	This is my husband/my wife.
Buone vacanze!	*[bwoh-neh vah-cahn-tzeh]*	Enjoy your holiday!
Qual è il suo/ tuo...? (inf)	*[qwal eh eel soo-oh/too-oh]*	What's your...?
...indirizzo	*[een-dee-ree-tsoh]*	...address
...indirizzo e-mail	*[een-dee-ree-tsoh ee-meh-eel]*	...email address
...numero di telefono	*[noo-meh-roh dee the-leh-foh-noh]*	...phone number

Listen to track 15

Che lavoro fa/ fai (inf)?	*[keh lah-voh-roh fah/fah-ee]*	What's your occupation?
Sono un medico.	*[soh-noh oon meh-dee-coh]*	I'm a doctor.

Di dove sei? / Da dove viene/ vieni (inf)?	[dee doh-veh seh-ee] / [dah doh-veh vee-eh-neh/vee-eh-nee]	Where are you from?
Sono inglese, vengo da Londra.	[soh-noh een-gleh-seh, vehn-goh dah lohn-drah]	I am English, from London.
Vengo...	[vehn-goh]	I'm...
...dall' Australia/dal Canada/dall' Inghilterra/ dalla Nuova Zelanda	[dah-lah-oo-strah-lee-ah/dahl cah-nah-dah /dahl-een-gyeel-tehr-rah/dah-lah nwoh-vah zeh-lahn-dah]	...from Australia/from Canada/from England/from New Zealand
...dagli Stati Uniti	[dah-lee stah-tee oo-nee-tee]	...from the USA

Listen to track 16

Lei è sposato/ sposata? (m/f) / Sei sposato/ sposata ? (m/f) inf	[leh-ee eh spoh-sah-toh/spoh-sah-tah] [seh-ee spoh-sah-toh / spoh-sah-tah]	Are you married?
Sono sposato/ sposata. (m/f)	[soh-noh spoh-sah-toh/spoh-sah-tah]	I'm married.

Sono single.	*[soh-noh seen-gohl]*	I'm single.
Quanti anni...	*[qwan-tee ahn-nee]*	How old...
...ha lei?/hai tu? (inf)	*[ah le-ee/ah-ee too]*	...are you?
...è sua figlia?	*[eh soo-ah fee-lya]*	...is your daughter?
...è suo figlio?	*[eh soo-oh fee-lyoh]*	...is your son?
Ho ... anni.	*[hoh ... ahn-nee]*	I'm ... years old.
Ha ... anni.	*[hah ... ahn-nee]*	He/She is ... years old.
Io (non) sono...	*[ee-oh (nohn) soh-noh]*	I'm (not)...
Lei è...? / Tu sei...? (inf)	*[leh-ee eh / too seh-ee]*	Are you...?

Listen to track 17

fidanzato	*[fee-dahn-zah-toh]*	boyfriend
fratello	*[frah-tehl-loh]*	brother
figlia	*[fee-lya]*	daughter
padre	*[pah-dreh]*	father
amico/amica (m/f)	*[ah-mee-coh/ ah-mee-cah]*	friend
fidanzata	*[fee-dahn-zah-tah]*	girlfriend
marito	*[mah-ree-toh]*	husband
madre	*[mah-dreh]*	mother

compagno/ compagna (m/f)	*[cohm-pah-nyoh/cohm-pah-nyah]*	partner
sorella	*[soh-reh-lah]*	sister
figlio	*[fee-lyoh]*	son
moglie	*[moh-lee-eh]*	wife

Listen to track 18

Questo è...	*[qwes-toh eh]*	Here's...
...mio fratello	*[mee-oh frah-teh-loh]*	...my brother
...il mio amico / la mia amica (m/f)	*[eel mee-oh ah-mee-coh / lah mee-ah ah-mee-cah]*	...my friend
...mia moglie	*[mee-ah moh-lee-eh]*	...my wife
...mio marito	*[mee-oh mah-ree-toh]*	...my husband
...mia sorella	*[mee-ah soh-rehl-lah]*	...my sister
...mia figlia	*[mee-ah fee-lyah]*	...my daughter
...mio figlio	*[mee-oh fee-lyoh]*	...my son
...il mio bambino	*[eel mee-oh bahm-bee-noh]*	...my child

Listen to track 19

il ragazzo	*[eel rah-gah-tsoh]*	the boy

la ragazza	[lah rah-gah-tsah]	the girl
l'uomo	[lwo-moh]	the man
la donna	[lah dohn-nah]	the woman
felice	[feh-lee-cheh]	happy
triste	[tree-steh]	sad
Potrebbe...?	[poh-treh-beh]	Could you...?
Per favore...	[pehr fah-voh-reh]	Please...
...ripetilo.	[ree-peh-tee-loh]	...repeat that.

Listen to track 20

Vorrei augurarle... / Vorrei augurarti... (inf)	[vohr-rey ah-oo-goo-rahr-leh / vohr-rey ah-oo-goo-rahr-tee]	I'd like to wish you...
...Felice anno nuovo!	[feh-lee-cheh ahn-noh nwo-voh]	...Happy New Year!
...Buona Pasqua!	[bwoh-nah pahs-qwah]	...Happy Easter!
...Buon compleanno!	[bwon cohm-pleh-ahn-noh]	...Happy birthday!
Buon viaggio!	[bwon vyah-joh]	Have a good trip!

Chapter 4: Getting to know somebody / Fare conoscenza

Listen to track 21

Quanti anni ha? / Quanti anni hai? (inf)	*[qwahn-tee ahn-nee ah / qwahn-tee ahn-nee ha-ee]*	How old are you?
Io ho ... anni.	*[ee-oh hoh ... ahn-nee]*	I'm ... years old.
Lei è Italiano/ Italiana (m/f)? / Sei Italiano/ Italiana (m/f)? (inf)	*[leh-ee eh ee-tah-lyah-noh/ ee-tah-lyah-nah] / [seh-ee ee-tah-lyah-noh/ee-tah-lyah-nah]*	Are you Italian?
Io sono Inglese/ Scozzese/ Americano.	*[ee-oh soh-noh een-gleh-seh/ scoh-tzeh-seh/ ah-meh-ree-cah-noh]*	I'm English/ Scottish/ American.
Dove vive?	*[doh-veh vee-veh]*	Where do you live?
Dove vivi? (inf) / Dove vivete? (pl)	*[doh-veh vee-vee] / [doh-veh vee-veh-teh]*	Where do you live?
Io vivo a Londra.	*[ee-oh vee-voh ah lohn-drah]*	I live in London.
Noi viviamo a Glasgow.	*[noh-ee vee-vee-ah-moh ah glas-gow]*	We live in Glasgow.

Listen to track 22

Io sono...	*[ee-oh soh-noh]*	I'm...
...single	*[seen-gohl]*	...single
...sposato/a (m/f)	*[spoh-sah-toh/spoh-sah-tah]*	...married
...divorziato/a (m/f)	*[dee-vohr-tsyah-toh/ dee-vohr-tsyah-tah]*	... divorced
Io ho...	*[ee-oh hoh]*	I have...
...un ragazzo	*[oon rah-gah-tsoh]*	...a boyfriend
...una ragazza	*[oonah rah-gah-tsah]*	...a girlfriend
...un compagno/ una compagna (m/f)	*[oon cohm-pah-nyoh/ oonah cohm-pah-nyah]*	...a partner (male/female)
...figli	*[fee-lee]*	...children

Listen to track 23

Non ho figli.	*[nohn hoh fee-lee]*	I have no children.
Sono qui in vacanza/per affari/per il fine settimana.	*[soh-noh qwee een vah-cahn-tsah/pehr ah-fah-ree/pehr eel fee-neh seht-tee-mah-nah]*	I'm here on holiday/on business/for the weekend.

Che lavoro fa? / Che lavoro fai? (inf)	*[keh lah-voh-roh fah / keh lah-voh-roh fah-ee]*	What work do you do?
Io sono...	*[ee-oh soh-noh]*	I'm...
...un medico	*[oon meh-dee-coh]*	...a doctor
...un manager	*[oon mah-nah-jer]*	...a manager
Lavoro da casa.	*[lah-voh-roh dah cah-sah]*	I work from home.
Sono un lavoratore autonomo.	*[soh-noh oon lah-voh-rah-toh-reh ah-oo-toh-noh-moh]*	I'm self-employed.

Part 3: On the go: Direction and transportation / Spostamenti: Direzione e trasporto

There is nothing worse than feeling lost, let alone being lost in a foreign country. Learning Italian has, of course, some very practical uses when you are in Italy. When traveling, having a basic understanding of how to ask for directions or simply knowing the words for public transportation can make all the difference in your experience.

Chapter 5: Asking for direction / Chiedere la direzione

Listen to track 24

Mi scusi, come si arriva alla stazione?	*[mee scoo-see, coh-meh see ah-ree-vah ahl-lah stah-tsyoh-neh]*	Excuse me, how do I get to the station?
Prosegua dritto, dopo la chiesa giri a sinistra/destra.	*[proh-seh-gwah dreet-toh, doh-poh lah kee-eh-sah jee-ree ah see-nees-trah/dehs-trah]*	Keep straight on, after the church turn left/right.
È lontano?	*[eh lohn-tah-noh]*	Is it far?
No, 200 metri/ cinque minuti.	*[noh, doo-eh-chen-toh meh-tree/ cheen-qweh mee-noo-tee]*	No, 200 yards/ five minutes.
Grazie!	*[grah-tsyeh]*	Thank you!
Noi stiamo cercando...	*[noh-ee stee-ah-moh cher-cahn-doh]*	We're looking for...
Possiamo andarci a piedi?	*[pohs-see-ah-moh ahn-dahr-cee ah pyeh-dee]*	Can we walk there?
Ci siamo persi.	*[cee see-ah-moh pehr-see]*	We're lost.

È questa la direzione giusta per...?	*[eh qwes-tah lah dee-reh-tsee-oh-neh djoos-stah pehr]*	Is this the right way to...?
Può indicarmelo sulla cartina?	*[pwoh een-dee-cahr-meh-loh sool-lah cahr-tee-nah]*	Can you show me on the map?

Listen to track 25

C'è la segnaletica.	*[cheh lah seh-nyah-leh-tee-cah]*	It's signposted.
È all'angolo della strada.	*[eh ahl-lahn-goh-loh dehl-lah strah-dah]*	It's on the corner of the street.
E' laggiù.	*[eh lah-djoo]*	It's over there.
di fronte a	*[dee fron-teh ah]*	opposite from
accanto a	*[ah-cahn-toh]*	next to
vicino a	*[vee-chee-noh ah]*	near to
incrocio	*[een-croh-tchoh]*	crossroad
rotatoria	*[roh-tah-toh-ryah]*	roundabout

Chapter 6: Taking the bus / Prendere l'autobus

Listen to track 26

Mi scusi, quale autobus porta in centro?	*[mee scoo-see, qwah-leh ah-oo-toh-boos pohr-tah een chen-troh]*	Excuse me, which bus goes to the center?
Il 780.	*[eel seht-teh-chen-toh-oh-tahn-tah]*	Number 780.
Dov'è la fermata dell'autobus?	*[doh-veh lah fehr-mah-tah dehl-lah-oo-toh-boos]*	Where is the bus stop?
Lì, sulla sinistra.	*[lee, sool-lah see-nees-trah]*	There, on the left.
Dove posso comprare i biglietti per l'autobus?	*[doh-veh pohs-soh cohm-prah-reh ee bee-lee-eht-tee pehr lah-oo-toh-boos]*	Where can I buy bus tickets?
Lì giù, alla biglietteria automatica.	*[lee joo, ahl-lah bee-lee-eht-teh-ree-ah ah-oo-toh-mah-tee-cah]*	Over there, at the ticket machine.
C'è un autobus per...?	*[cheh oon ah-oo-toh-boos pehr]*	Is there a bus to...?

| Dove posso prendere l'autobus per...? | *[doh-veh pohs-soh prehn-deh-reh lah-oo-toh-boos pehr]* | Where do I catch the bus to go to...? |

Listen to track 27

Quanto costa andare... ?	*[qwan-toh coh-stah ahn-dah-reh]*	How much is it to... ?
...in centro	*[een chen-troh]*	...to the center
...in spiaggia	*[een spya-jya]*	...to the beach
...al centro commerciale	*[ahl chen-troh com-mehr-cha-leh]*	...to the shops
...al Colosseo	*[ahl coh-lohs-seh-oh]*	...to the Colosseum
Ogni quanto passano gli autobus per...?	*[oh-nyee qwahn-toh pahs-sah-noh lee ah-oo-toh-boos pehr...]*	How frequent are the buses to...?
Quando parte il primo/l'ultimo autobus per...?	*[qwahn-doh pahr-teh eel pree-moh/lool-tee-moh ah-oo-toh-boos pehr]*	When is the first/last bus to...?
Può dirmi quando scendere?	*[pwoh deer-mee qwahn-doh shehn-deh-reh]*	Could you tell me when to get off?

Questa è la mia fermata.	*[qwehs-stah eh lah mee-ah fehr-mah-tah]*	This is my stop.
Prenda la metropolitana, è più veloce.	*[prehn-dah lah meh-troh-poh-lee-tah-nah, eh pyoo veh-loh-cheh]*	Take the metro, it's quicker.

Chapter 7: Traveling by metro / La metropolitana

entrata	*[ehn-trah-tah]*	entrance
uscita	*[oo-shee-tah]*	way out/exit sor-tee
linea della metropolitana	*[lee-neh-ah dehl-lah meh-troh-poh-lee-tah-nah]*	metro line
direzione...	*[dee-reh-tsyo-neh]*	in the direction of...
linea di collegamento	*[lee-neh-ah dee cohl-leh-gah-mehn-toh]*	connecting line
Dov'è la fermata della metro più vicina?	*[doh-veh lah fehr-mah-tah dehl-lah meh-troh pyoo vee-chee-nah]*	Where is the nearest metro?
Sto andando a...	*[stoh ahn-dahn-doh ah]*	I'm going to...
Come funziona la biglietteria automatica?	*[coh-meh foon-tsyo-nah lah bee-lee-eht-teh-ree-ah ah-oo-toh-mah-tee-cah]*	How does the ticket machine work?

Avete una cartina della metropolitana?	*[ah-veh-teh oo-nah cahr-tee-nah dehl-lah meh-troh-poh-lee-tah-nah]*	Do you have a map of the metro?
Come posso arrivare a...?	*[coh-meh pohs-soh ah-ree-vah-reh ah]*	How do I get to...?
Devo cambiare?	*[deh-voh cahm-byah-reh]*	Do I have to change?
Quale è la linea per...?	*[qwah-leh eh lah lee-neh-ah pehr]*	Which line is it for...?
In quale direzione?	*[een qwah-leh dee-reh-tsyoh-neh]*	In which direction?
Qual è la prossima fermata?	*[qwah-leh lah proh-see-mah fehr-mah-tah]*	What is the next stop?

Chapter 8: Traveling by train / Il treno

Listen to track 29

orari	*[oh-rah-ree]*	timetable
Domenica e festivi	*[doh-meh-nee-cah eh feh-stee-vee]*	Sundays and holidays
ai binari	*[ah-ee bee-nah-ree]*	access to the platforms
Quando parte il prossimo treno per...?	*[qwhan-doh pahr-teh eel proh-see-moh treh-noh pehr]*	When is the next train to...?
Alle cinque e dieci	*[ahl-le cheen-qweh eh dee-eh-chee]*	At ten past five
Due biglietti per...	*[doo-eh bee-lee-eh-tee pehr]*	Two tickets to...
Solo andata o andata e ritorno?	*[soh-loh ahn-dah-tah oh ahn-dah-tah eh ree-tohr-noh]*	Single (one-way) or return (round-trip)?
prima classe/ seconda classe	*[pree-mah clah-seh/seh-cohn-dah clah-seh]*	first class/second class
fumatori/non fumatori	*[foo-mah-toh-ree/nohn foo-mah-toh-ree]*	smoking/non-smoking

C'è un supplemento da pagare?	*[cheh oon soop-leh-mehn-toh dah pah-gah-reh]*	Is there a supplement to pay?
Vorrei un biglietto per il Frecciarossa per Milano.	*[voh-reh-ee oon bee-lee-eh-toh pehr eel freht-cha-rohs-sah pehr mee-lah-noh]*	I want to book a seat on the Frecciarossa to Milan.
Quando parte il treno per...?	*[qwahn-doh pahr-teh eel treh-noh pehr...]*	When is the train to...?

Listen to track 30

Quando parte?	*[qwahn-doh pahr-teh]*	When does it leave?
il primo/ l'ultimo	*[eel pree-moh/ lool-tee-moh]*	the first/the last
A che ora arriva a...?	*[ah keh oh-rah ah-ree-vah ah]*	When does it arrive in...?
Devo cambiare?	*[deh-voh cahm-byah-reh]*	Do I have to change?
A quale binario parte?	*[ah qwah-leh bee-nah-ree-oh pahr-teh]*	Which platform does it leave from?
Questo è il binario per il treno per Roma?	*[qwes-toh eh eel bee-nah-ree-oh pehr eel treh-noh pehr roh-mah]*	Is this the right platform for the train to Rome?

Questo è il treno per...?	*[qwes-toh eh eel treh-noh pehr]*	Is this the train for...?
Il treno ferma a...?	*[eel treh-noh fehr-mah ah]*	Does the train stop at...?
Dove posso cambiare per...?	*[doh-veh pohs-soh cahm-byah-reh pehr]*	Where do I change for...?
Per favore, può avvisarmi quando arriviamo a...?	*[pehr fah-voh-reh, pwoh ah-vee-sahr-mee qwan-doh ah-ree-vyah-moh ah]*	Please tell me when we get to...
Questo posto è libero?	*[qwes-toh poh-stoh eh lee-beh-roh]*	Is this seat free?

Chapter 9: Traveling by taxi / Il taxi

Listen to track 31

la stazione dei taxi	*[lah stah-tsyoh-neh deh-ee tah-xee]*	taxi rank
Vorrei un taxi.	*[voh-reh-ee oon tah-xee]*	I would like a taxi.
Dove posso prendere un taxi?	*[doh-veh pohs-soh prehn-deh-reh oon tah-xee]*	Where can I get a taxi?
Potrebbe chiamarmi un taxi?	*[poh-trehb-beh kee-ah-mahr-mee oon tah-xee]*	Could you order me a taxi?
Quanto costerà andare...?	*[qwahn-toh coh-steh-rah ahn-dah-reh]*	How much is it going to cost to go to...?
...in centro	*[een chen-troh]*	...to the town center
...in stazione	*[een stah-tsyoh-neh]*	...to the station
...all' aeroporto	*[ahl-lah-eh-roh-pohr-toh]*	...to the airport
...a questo indirizzo	*[ah qwehs-toh een-dee-reet-tsoh]*	...to this address
Quanto costa?	*[qwahn-toh coh-stah]*	How much is it?

Tenga il resto.	*[tehn-gah eel reh-stoh]*	Keep the change.
Mi scusi, non ho il resto.	*[mee scoo-see, nohn oh eel reh-stoh]*	Sorry, I don't have any change.
Vado di fretta.	*[vah-doh dee freht-tah]*	I'm in a hurry.
È lontano?	*[eh lohn-tah-noh]*	Is it far?

Chapter 10: Traveling by boat and ferry / Barca e traghetto

Listen to track 32

Quando parte il prossimo traghetto per...?	*[qwahn-doh pahr-the eel proh-see-moh trah-gueh-toh pehr]*	When is the next boat/ferry to...?
Avete gli orari?	*[ah-veh-teh lee oh-rah-ree]*	Do you have a timetable?
C'è un traghetto per auto per...?	*[cheh oon trah-gueh-toh pehr ah-oo-toh pehr]*	Is there a car ferry to...?
Quanto costa un biglietto di sola andata?	*[qwahn-toh coh-stah oon bee-lee-eh-toh dee soh-lah ahn-dah-tah]*	How much is a single (one-way)?
Quanto costa un biglietto andata e ritorno?	*[qwahn-toh coh-stah oon bee-lee-eh-toh ahn-dah-tah eh ree-tohr-noh]*	How much is a return (round-trip)?
un biglietto turistico	*[oon bee-lee-eh-toh too-rees-tee-coh]*	a tourist ticket
Quanto costa imbarcare un'auto e ... persone?	*[qwahn-toh coh-stah eem-bahr-cah-reh oon-ah-oo-toh eh ... pehr-soh-neh]*	How much is it for a car and ... people?

Quanto dura la traversata?	*[qwahn-toh doo-rah lah trah-vehr-sah-tah]*	How long is the crossing?
Da dove parte la barca?	*[dah doh-veh pahr-teh lah bahr-cah]*	Where does the boat leave from?
Quando parte la prima/ l'ultima barca?	*[qwahn-doh pahr-teh lah pree-mah/lool-tee-mah bahr-cah]*	When is the first/ last boat?
A che ora arriviamo a...?	*[ah keh oh-rah ahr-ree-vyah-moh ah]*	What time do we get to...?
C'è un posto dove mangiare sulla barca?	*[cheh oon poh-stoh doh-veh mahn-djah-reh sool-lah bahr-cah]*	Is there somewhere to eat on the boat?

Chapter 11: Air travel / Viaggio in aereo

Listen to track 33

Come posso raggiungere l'aeroporto?	*[coh-meh pohs-soh rah-djoon-djeh-reh lah-eh-roh-pohr-toh]*	How do I get to the airport?
Quanto tempo ci vuole per raggiungere l'aeroporto?	*[qwahn-toh tem-poh chee voo-oh-leh pehr rah-djoon-djeh-reh lah-eh-roh-pohr-toh]*	How long does it take to get to the airport?
Quanto costa il taxi fino...?	*[qwahn-toh coh-stah eel tah-xee fee-noh]*	How much is the taxi fare...?
...in città	*[een cheet-tah]*	...into town
...all'albergo	*[ahl-ahl-behr-goh]*	...to the hotel
C'è una navetta per andare in centro?	*[cheh oo-nah nah-veht-tah pehr ahn-dah-reh een chen-troh]*	Is there an airport bus to the city center?
Dove posso fare il check in?	*[doh-veh pohs-soh fah-reh eel check-een]*	Where do I check in?

Dove sono i bagagli del volo da...?	*[doh-veh soh-noh ee bah-gah-lee dehl voh-loh dah]*	Where is the luggage for the flight from...?
Da quale gate parte il volo per...?	*[dah qwah-leh gate pahr-the eel voh-loh pehr]*	Which is the departure gate for the flight to...?
L'imbarco avverrà al gate numero...	*[leem-bahr-coh ah-veh-rah ahl gate noo-meh-roh]*	Boarding will take place at gate number...
Vada subito al gate numero...	*[vah-dah soo-bee-toh ahl gate noo-meh-roh]*	Go immediately to gate number...
Il suo volo è in ritardo.	*[eel soo-oh voh-loh eh een ree-tahr-doh]*	Your flight is delayed.

Chapter 12: Immigration and customs / Immigrazione e dogana

Listen to track 34

controllo del passaporto	*[kohn-trohl-loh dehl pah-sah-pohr-toh]*	passport control
UE (Unione Europea)	*[oo-eh (oo-nyo-neh eh-oo-roh-peh-ah]*	EU (European Union)
altri passaporti	*[ahl-tree pah-sah-pohr-tee]*	other passports
dogana	*[doh-gah-nah]*	customs
Devo pagare una tassa per questo?	*[deh-voh-pah-gah-reh oo-nah tahs-sah pehr qwes-toh]*	Do I have to pay duty on this?
È per uso personale.	*[eh pehr oo-soh pehr-soh-nah-leh]*	It is for my own personal use.
Stiamo andando a...	*[stee-ah-moh ahn-dahn-doh ah]*	We are on our way to... (if in transit through a country)

Chapter 13: Petrol (Gas) / Rifornimento

Listen to track 35

benzina senza piombo	*[behn-zee-nah sehn-tsah pyom-boh]*	unleaded
diesel	*[dee-sehl]*	diesel
Il pieno, per favore.	*[eel pee-eh-noh, pehr fah-voh-reh]*	Fill it up, please.
Può controllare l'olio/l'acqua per favore?	*[pwoh cohn-trohl-lah-reh loh-lee-oh/ lah-qwah, pehr fah-voh-reh]*	Please check the oil/the water.
...euro di benzina senza piombo.	*[eh-oo-roh dee behn-zee-nah sehn-tsah pyom-boh]*	...euros' worth of unleaded petrol (gas).
Pompa di benzina numero...	*[pohm-pah dee behn-zee-nah noo-meh-roh]*	Pump number...
Può controllare la pressione delle gomme?	*[pwoh cohn-trohl-lah-reh lah press-see-oh-neh dehl-leh gohm-meh]*	Can you check the tire pressure?
Dove posso pagare?	*[doh-veh pohs-soh pah-gah-reh]*	Where do I pay?
Accettate carte di credito?	*[ah-tchet-tah-teh cahr-teh dee creh-dee-toh]*	Do you take credit cards?

Chapter 14: Breakdowns and repairs / Avarie e riparazioni

Listen to track 36

assistenza in caso di guasto	*[ah-see-stehn-zah een cah-soh dee gwah-stoh]*	breakdown assistance
Può aiutarmi?	*[pwoh ah-yoo-tahr-mee]*	Can you help me?
La mia auto è in panne.	*[lah mee-ah ah-oo-toh eh een pahn-neh]*	My car has broken down.
Non riesco a far partire l'auto.	*[nohn ree-eh-scoh ah fahr pahr-tee-reh lah-oo-toh]*	I can't start the car.
Ho finito la benzina.	*[oh fee-nee-toh lah behn-zee-nah]*	I've run out of petrol (gas).
C'è un'officina qui vicino?	*[cheh oon-off-fee-chee-nah qwee vee-chee-noh]*	Is there a garage near here?
Può rimorchiarmi all'officina più vicina?	*[pwoh ree-mohr-kyahr-mee ahl-off-fee-chee-nah pyoo vee-chee-nah]*	Can you tow me to the nearest garage?

Avete dei pezzi di ricambio per una...?	*[ah-veh-the deh-ee peh-tsee dee ree-cahm-byoh pehr oon-ah]*	Do you have parts for a ... (make of car)?
C'è qualcosa che non va con il/la/lo...	*[cheh qwal-coh-sah keh nohn vah cohn eel/lah/loh]*	There's something wrong with the...

Chapter 15: Car parts / Pezzi di ricambio

Listen to track 37

Il/lo/la ... non funziona.	*[eel/loh/lah ... nohn foon-tsyoh-nah]*	The ... doesn't work.
I/Le ... non funzionano.	*[ee/leh ... nohn foon-tsyoh-nah-noh]*	The ... don't work.
l'acceleratore	*[lah-tche-leh-rah-toh-reh]*	accelerator
la batteria	*[lah baht-teh-ree-ah]*	battery
il cofano	*[eel coh-fah-noh]*	bonnet (hood)
i freni	*[ee freh-nee]*	brakes
lo starter	*[loh stahr-tehr]*	choke
la frizione	*[lah free-tsyoh-neh]*	clutch
il motore	*[eel moh-toh-reh]*	engine
il tubo di scarico	*[eel too-boh dee scah-ree-coh]*	exhaust pipe
il fusibile	*[eel foo-see-bee-leh]*	fuse
ingranaggi	*[een-grah-nah-djee]*	gears
il freno a mano	*[eel freh-noh ah mah-noh]*	handbrake
i fari	*[ee fah-ree]*	headlights
l'accensione	*[lah-tchen-tsyoh-neh]*	ignition

Listen to track 38

il lampeggiante	*[eel lahm-peh-djahn-teh]*	blinker/turn signal
il radiatore	*[eel rah-dyah-toh-reh]*	radiator
luci di retromarcia	*[loo-chee dee reh-troh-mahr-cha]*	reversing lights
cintura di sicurezza	*[cheen-too-rah dee see-coo-reh-tsah]*	seat belt
luci di posizione	*[loo-chee dee poh-see-tsyoh-neh]*	sidelights
ruota di scorta	*[roo-oh-tah dee scohr-tah]*	spare wheel
candele	*[cahn-deh-leh]*	spark plugs
sterzo	*[stehr-tsoh]*	steering
volante	*[voh-lahn-teh]*	steering wheel
il pneumatico	*[eel pneh-oo-mah-tee-coh]*	tire
ruota	*[roo-oh-tah]*	wheel
parabrezza	*[pah-rah-breh-tsah]*	windscreen (windshield)
rondelle del parabrezza	*[rohn-dehl-leh dehl pah-rah-breh-tsah]*	windscreen (windshield) washers
tergicristallo	*[tehr-gee-kree-stahl-loh]*	windscreen (windshield) wiper

Chapter 16: Road signs / Segnali stradali

Listen to track 39

Dogana	*[doh-gah-nah]*	Customs
stazione di pedaggio per l'autostrada	*[stah-tsyoh-neh dee peh-dah-djoh pehr lah-oo-toh-strah-dah]*	toll station for motorway
dare la precedenza	*[dah-reh lah preh-cheh-dehn-tsah]*	give way
rallentare	*[rahl-lehn-tah-reh]*	slow down
senso unico	*[sehn-soh oo-nee-coh]*	one way
deviazione	*[deh-vee-ah-tsyoh-neh]*	detour
Nord	*[nord]*	North
Sud	*[sood]*	South
Ovest	*[oh-vehst]*	West
Est	*[ehst]*	East
libero	*[lee-beh-roh]*	spaces
pieno	*[pyeh-noh]*	full
divieto di parcheggio	*[dee-vee-eh-toh dee pahr-ke-djoh]*	no parking
accendere i fari	*[ah-tchen-deh-reh ee fah-ree]*	switch on your light
autostrada	*[ah-oo-toh-strah-dah]*	motorway

Chapter 17: Signs and notices / Segnali e avvisi

Listen to track 40

ingresso	*[een-grehs-soh]*	entrance
uscita	*[oo-shee-tah]*	exit
aperto	*[ah-pehr-toh]*	open
chiuso	*[kee-oo-soh]*	closed
caldo	*[cahl-doh]*	hot
freddo	*[freh-doh]*	cold
tirare	*[tee-rah-reh]*	pull
spingere	*[speen-dje-reh]*	push
destra	*[deh-strah]*	right
sinistra	*[see-nee-strah]*	left
acqua potabile	*[ah-qwah poh-tah-bee-leh]*	drinking water
da asporto/da portar via	*[dah ah-spohr-toh/dah pohr-tahr vee-ah]*	take-away
degustazione di vini	*[deh-goo-stah-tsyoh-neh dee vee-nee]*	wine tasting
si prega di...	*[see preh-gah dee]*	Please...
libero	*[lee-beh-roh]*	free/vacant
occupato	*[oh-coo-pah-toh]*	engaged

Listen to track 41

cassa	_[cahs-sah]_	cashier
bagni	_[bah-nyee]_	toilets
donne	_[dohn-neh]_	ladies
uomini	_[woh-mee-nee]_	gents
fuori servizio	_[fwoh-ree sehr-vee-tsyoh]_	out of order
in affitto/a noleggio	_[een ah-feet-toh/ah-noh-leh-joh]_	for hire/to rent
in vendita	_[een vehn-dee-tah]_	for sale
divieto di balneazione	_[dee-vee-eh-toh dee bahl-neh-ah-tsyoh-neh]_	no bathing
seminterrato	_[seh-meen-teh-rah-toh]_	basement
piano terra	_[pyah-noh tehr-rah]_	ground floor
ascensore	_[ah-shen-soh-reh]_	lift
accesso ai treni	_[ah-ches-soh ah-ee treh-nee]_	access to the trains
camere disponibili	_[cah-meh-reh dees-poh-nee-bee-lee]_	rooms available
al completo	_[ahl cohmp-leh-toh]_	no vacancies

Listen to track 42

uscita di emergenza	*[oo-shee-tah dee eh-mehr-djehn-tsah]*	emergency exit
suonare	*[soo-oh-nah-reh]*	ring
premere	*[preh-meh-reh]*	press
privato	*[pree-vah-toh]*	private
stop	*[stohp]*	stop
biglietti	*[bee-lee-eht-tee]*	tickets
informazioni (pl)	*[een-for-mah-tsyoh-nee]*	information
convalida il tuo biglietto	*[cohn-vah-lee-dah eel too-oh bee-lee-eh-toh]*	validate your ticket
snack	*[snehk]*	snacks
deposito bagagli	*[deh-poh-see-toh bah-gah-lyee]*	left luggage
non fumatori	*[nohn foo-mah-toh-ree]*	non-smoking
fumatori	*[foo-mah-toh-ree]*	smoking
vietato fumare	*[vee-eh-tah-toh foo-mah-reh]*	no smoking

Part 4: Leisure, culture, and entertainment / Tempo libero, cultura, intrattenimento

One of the wonderful aspects of learning a language is the cultural immersion and the experiences you gain from it. Italian culture has a wealth of connections to leisure and entertainment, which can really enhance your level of enjoyment when learning the language. When you take your interests such as sports or the arts and apply them to learning Italian, you will find that you are more motivated and interested in increasing your knowledge about that topic while also learning the language along the way.

Chapter 18: Sightseeing and tourist office / Escursioni ed ufficio turistico

Listen to track 43

Dov'è l'ufficio turistico?	*[doh-veh loof-fee-tcho too-rees-tee-coh]*	Where is the tourist office?
Vorrei una guida che parli inglese.	*[voh-reh-ee oo-nah gwee-dah keh pahr-lee een-gleh-seh]*	I would like a guide who speaks English.
Cosa c'è da visitare nella zona?	*[coh-sah cheh dah vee-see-tah-reh nehl-lah zoh-nah]*	What is there to visit in the area?
Qual è il costo orario/ giornaliero?	*[qwah-leh eel coh-stoh oh-rah-ryoh/ djohr-nah-lee-eh-roh]*	What is the charge per hour/ day?
Avete dei volantini?	*[ah-veh-the deh-ee voh-lahn-tee-nee]*	Do you have any leaflets?
Ci sono delle escursioni?	*[chee soh-noh dehl-leh eh-scoor-see-oh-nee]*	Are there any excursions?
Vorremmo andare a...	*[voh-reh-moh ahn-dah-reh ah]*	We'd like to go to...

Listen to track 44

Sono interessato alla pittura.	*[soh-noh een-teh-rehs-sah-toh ahl-lah peet-too-rah]*	I am interested in painting.
scultura	*[scool-too-rah]*	sculpture
architettura	*[ahr-kee-teh-too-rah]*	architecture
il castello	*[eel cahs-tell-loh]*	the castle
la cattedrale	*[lah cah-teh-drah-leh]*	the cathedral
la chiesa	*[lah kee-eh-sah]*	the church
il museo	*[eel moo-seh-oh]*	the museum
il monastero	*[eel moh-nah-steh-roh]*	the monastery
il monumento	*[eel moh-noo-mehn-toh]*	the monument
il centro storico	*[eel chen-troh stoh-ree-coh]*	the old city
il palazzo	*[eel pah-lah-tsoh]*	the palace
le rovine	*[leh roh-veeh-neh]*	the ruins
lo stadio	*[loh stah-dee-oh]*	the stadium
le statue	*[leh stah-too-eh]*	the statues
la piazza centrale	*[lah pee-ah-tsah chen-trah-leh]*	the main square

Listen to track 45

Quanto costa entrare?	*[qwahn-toh coh-stah ehn-trah-reh]*	How much does it cost to get in?
Quanto costa l'ingresso?	*[qwahn-toh coh-stah leen-grehs-soh]*	What is the price of admission?
C'è una riduzione per i bambini/gli studenti?	*[cheh oo-nah ree-doo-tsyoh-neh pehr ee bahm-bee-nee/ lee stoo-dehn-tee]*	Is there a discount for children/ students?
Ci sono riduzioni per...?	*[chee soh-noh ree-doo-tsyoh-nee pehr]*	Are there any reductions for...?
...i bambini	*[ee bahm-bee-nee]*	...children
...gli studenti	*[lee stoo-dehn-tee]*	...students
...i disoccupati	*[ee dee-soh-coo-pah-tee]*	...the unemployed
...gli anziani	*[lee ahn-tsyah-nee]*	...senior citizens
A che ora...?	*[ah keh oh-rah]*	What time does it...?
...chiude	*[kyoo-deh]*	...close
...apre	*[ah-preh]*	...open
Dov'è l'entrata/ uscita?	*[doh-veh lehn-trah-tah/oo-shee-tah]*	Where is the entrance/exit?

Listen to track 46

Vorrei...	[voh-reh-ee]	I'd like ...
...un catalogo	[oon cah-tah-loh-goh]	...a catalogue
...una guida	[oo-nah-gwee-dah]	...a guide
...una cartina	[oo-nah cahr-tee-nah]	...a local map
Vorrei vedere...	[vohr-reh-ee veh-deh-reh]	I'd like to see...
Cos'è quello?	[coh-seh qwehl-loh]	What's that?
Posso fare delle foto?	[poh-soh fah-reh dehl-leh foh-toh]	Can I take photos?
Quando c'è il prossimo...?	[qwahn-doh cheh eel prohs-see-moh]	When's the next...?
...giro/visita	[gee-roh/vee-see-tah]	...tour
...l'escursione giornaliera	[leh-scoor-see-oh-neh djohr-nah-lee-eh-rah]	...day trip excursion
È incluso l'alloggio?	[eh een-cloo-soh lahl-loh-djoh]	Is the accomodation included?
il biglietto di ingresso	[eel bee-lee-eh-toh deen-grehs-soh]	the admission charge
il cibo	[eel chee-boh]	food

il trasporto	*[eel trahs-pohr-toh]*	transport
Quanto dura la visita?	*[qwahn-toh doo-rah lah vee-see-tah]*	How long is the tour?
A che ora dovremmo tornare?	*[ah keh oh-rah doh-vrehm-moh tohr-nah-reh]*	What time should we be back?

Chapter 19: Fun and entertainment / Divertimento ed intrattenimento

Listen to track 47

Cosa c'è da fare la sera?	*[coh-sah cheh dah fah-reh lah seh-rah]*	What is there to do in the evenings?
Avete una lista di eventi per questo mese?	*[ah-veh-teh oo-nah lees-tah dee eh-vehn-tee pehr qwes-toh meh-seh]*	Do you have a list of events for this month?
C'è qualcosa da fare per i bambini?	*[cheh qwal-coh-sah dah fah-reh pehr ee bahm-bee-nee]*	Is there anything for children to do?
Dove posso/ possiamo...?	*[doh-veh pohs-soh/pohs-see-ah-moh]*	Where can I/ we...?
andare a pesca	*[ahn-dah-reh ah pehs-cah]*	go fishing
andare a cavallo	*[ahn-dah-reh ah cah-vahl-loh]*	go riding
Ci sono delle buone spiagge di sabbia qui vicino?	*[chee soh-noh dehl-leh bwoh-neh spee-ah-djeh dee sa-bee-ah qwee vee-chee-noh]*	Are there any good (sandy) beaches near here?
C'è una piscina?	*[cheh oo-nah pee-shee-nah]*	Is there a swimming pool?

Chapter 20: Music / La musica

Listen to track 48

Ci sono dei buoni concerti?	*[chee soh-noh deh-ee bwoh-nee cohn-cher-tee]*	Are there any good concerts on?
Dove posso acquistare i biglietti per il concerto?	*[doh-veh pohs-soh ah-qwee-stah-reh ee bee-lee-eh-tee pehr eel cohn-cher-toh]*	Where can I get tickets for the concert?
Dove possiamo ascoltare della musica classica/del jazz?	*[doh-veh pohs-see-ah-moh ah-scohl-tah-reh dehl-lah moo-see-cah clah-see-cah/ dehl jazz]*	Where can we hear some classical music/ jazz?
Mi piace ascoltare musica.	*[mee pyah-cheh ah-scohl-tah-reh moo-see-cah]*	I love listening to music.
Che genere di musica ascolti?	*[keh djeh-neh-reh dee moo-see-cah ah-scohl-tee]*	What kind of music do you listen to?
Sono un musicista.	*[soh-noh oon moo-see-chee-stah]*	I'm a musician.

Io sono direttore d'orchestra.	*[ee-oh soh-noh dee-reht-toh-reh dohr-keh-strah]*	I'm a conductor.
Sono un/una cantante.	*[soh-noh oon/ oo-nah cahn-tahn-teh]*	I'm a singer.
Io canto.	*[ee-oh cahn-toh]*	I sing.

Listen to track 49

Io suono...	*[ee-oh soo-oh-noh]*	I play...
...il pianoforte	*[eel pyah-noh-fohr-teh]*	...the piano
...il pianoforte a coda	*[eel pyah-noh-fohr-teh ah coh-dah]*	...grand piano
...la chitarra classica	*[lah kee-tahr-rah clah-see-cah]*	...classical guitar
...la chitarra elettrica	*[lah kee-tahr-rah eh-let-tree-cah]*	...electric guitar
...il violino	*[eel vee-oh-lee-noh]*	...violin
...il violoncello	*[eel vee-oh-lohn-chel-loh]*	...cello
...il mandolino	*[eel mahn-doh-lee-noh]*	...mandolin
...l'arpa	*[lahr-pah]*	...harp

...la batteria	*[lah baht-teh-ree-ah]*	...drums
...il basso	*[eel bahs-soh]*	...bass guitar
...il contrabbasso	*[eel cohn-trah-bah-soh]*	...double bass
...il fagotto	*[eel fah-goht-toh]*	...bassoon
...il flauto	*[eel flah-oo-toh]*	...flute
...il clarinetto	*[eel clah-ree-neht-toh]*	...clarinet
...il sassofono	*[eel sahs-soh-foh-noh]*	...saxophone
...la tromba	*[lah trohm-bah]*	...trumpet

Chapter 21: Cinema / Il cinema

Listen to track 50

sottotitolato	*[soht-toh-tee-toh-lah-toh]*	subtitled
spettacolo	*[speht-tah-coh-loh]*	performance
in lingua originale (non doppiato)	*[een leen-gwa oh-ree-jee-nah-leh (nohn dop-pyah-toh)]*	in the original language (i.e. not dubbed)
Cosa c'è al cinema?	*[coh-sah cheh ahl chee-neh-mah]*	What's on at the cinema?
Quando inizia/ finisce il film?	*[qwahn-doh ee-nee-tsya/ fee-nee-sheh eel feel-m]*	When does the film start/finish?
Quanto costano i biglietti?	*[qwahn-toh coh-stah-noh ee bee-lee-eh-tee]*	How much are the tickets?
Vorrei due posti da ... euro.	*[vohr-re-ee doo-eh poh-stee dah ... eh-oo-roh]*	I'd like two seats at ... euros.

Chapter 22: Theater and opera / Il teatro e l'opera

Listen to track 51

lo spettacolo	*[loh speht-tah-coh-loh]*	play
lo spettacolo	*[loh speht-tah-coh-loh]*	performance
in platea (fossa dell'orchestra)	*[een plah-teh-ah (foh-sa deh-lohr-ke-stra)]*	in the stalls (orchestra seats)
in galleria (balconata)	*[een gahl-leh-ree-ah (bahl-ko-na-ta)]*	in the gallery (balcony)
il posto/la poltrona	*[eel poh-stoh/ lah pohl-troh-nah]*	seat
il guardaroba	*[eel-gwar-dah-roh-bah]*	cloakroom
intervallo	*[een-tehr-vahl-loh]*	intermission
Cosa c'è a teatro/ all'opera?	*[coh-sah cheh ah teh-ah-troh/ahl-loh-peh-rah]*	What is on at the theater/at the opera?
Quanto costano i biglietti?	*[qwahn-toh coh-stah-noh ee bee-lee-eh-tee]*	What prices are the tickets?
Vorrei due biglietti...	*[voh-reh-ee doo-eh bee-lee-eh-tee]*	I'd like two tickets...

...per questa sera	*[pehr qwes-tah seh-rah]*	...for tonight
...per domani sera	*[pehr doh-mah-nee seh-rah]*	...for tomorrow night
...per il cinque Agosto	*[peh eel cheen-qweh ah-goh-stoh]*	...for 5th August
Quando inizia/ finisce lo spettacolo?	*[qwahn-doh ee-nee-tsyah/ fee-nee-sheh loh speht-tah-coh-loh]*	When does the performance begin/end?

Chapter 23: Television / La televisione

telecomando	_[teh-leh-coh-mahn-doh]_	remote control
telenovela/ soap opera	_[teh-leh-noh-veh-lah/soap opera]_	soap
notiziario	_[noh-tee-tsyah-ree-oh]_	news
accendere	_[ah-tchen-deh-reh]_	to switch on
spegnere	_[speh-nee-eh-reh]_	to switch off
i cartoni animati	_[ee cahr-toh-nee ah-nee-mah-tee]_	cartoons
Dov'è la televisione?	_[doh-veh lah teh-leh-vee-see-oh-neh]_	Where is the television?
Come si accende?	_[coh-meh see ah-tchen-deh]_	How do you switch it on?
Cosa c'è in televisione?	_[coh-sah cheh een teh-leh-vee-see-oh-neh]_	What is on television?
A che ora c'è il notiziario?	_[ah ke oh-rah cheh eel noh-tee-tsyah-ree-oh]_	When is the news?

Avete dei canali in lingua inglese?	*[ah-veh-teh deh-ee cah-nah-lee een leen-gwah een-gleh-seh]*	Do you have any English language channels?
Avete dei video in Inglese?	*[ah-veh-teh deh-ee vee-deh-oh een een-gleh-seh]*	Do you have any English videos?

Chapter 24: Sports / Lo sport

Listen to track 53

Dove posso/ possiamo...?	*[doh-veh pohs-soh/pohs-see-ah-moh]*	Where can I/ we...?
giocare a calcio	*[djoh-cah-reh ah cahl-tcho]*	play soccer
giocare a tennis	*[djoh-cah-reh ah ten-nees]*	play tennis
giocare a golf	*[djoh-cah-reh ah golf]*	play golf
nuotare	*[nwoh-tah-reh]*	go swimming
fare jogging	*[fah-reh jogging]*	go jogging
Qual è il costo orario?	*[qwal-eh eel coh-stoh oh-rah-ree-oh]*	How much is it per hour?
Bisogna essere soci?	*[bee-soh-nya ehs-seh-reh soh-chee]*	Do you have to be a member?
Possiamo noleggiare...?	*[pohs-see-ah-moh noh-leh-djah-reh]*	Can we hire (rent)...?
...racchette	*[rahk-keht-teh]*	...rackets
...mazze da golf	*[mah-tseh dah golf]*	...golf clubs

Vorremmo andare a vedere la ... giocare.	*[voh-rehm-moh ahn-dah-reh ah veh-deh-reh lah ... djoh-cah-reh]*	We'd like to go to see (name of team) play.
Dove posso/ possiamo prendere i biglietti?	*[doh-veh pohs-soh/pohs-syah-moh prehn-deh-reh ee bee-lee-eh-tee]*	Where can I/we get tickets?
Non ci sono più biglietti per la partita.	*[nohn chee soh-noh pyoo bee-lee-eh-tee pehr lah pahr-tee-tah]*	There are no tickets left for the game.

Listen to track 54

Quale sport pratichi?	*[qwa-leh sport prah-tee-kee]*	What sports do you play?
tiro con l'arco	*[tee-roh cohn lahr-coh]*	archery
ciclismo	*[cheek-lees-moh]*	cycling
pallavolo	*[pahl-lah-voh-loh]*	volleyball
pallacanestro	*[pahl-lah-cah-neh-stroh]*	basketball
freccette	*[freh-tcheh-teh]*	darts
sci	*[shee]*	skiing
palla	*[pahl-lah]*	ball
scacchi	*[scah-kee]*	chess
dama	*[dah-mah]*	draughts (checkers)

Listen to track 55

carte	*[cahr-teh]*	cards
cuori	*[qwoh-ree]*	hearts
fiori	*[fyoh-ree]*	clubs
picche	*[peek-keh]*	spades
quadri	*[qwah-dree]*	diamonds
tocca a te	*[toh-kah ah teh]*	your turn
gioco da tavolo	*[djoh-coh dah tah-voh-loh]*	board game
gioco	*[djoh-coh]*	game
partita	*[pahr-tee-tah]*	match
punteggio	*[poon-teh-djoh]*	score
vincitore	*[veen-chee-toh-reh]*	winner
arbitro	*[ahr-bee-troh]*	referee

Chapter 25: Walking / La passeggiata

Listen to track 56

Ci sono delle passeggiate guidate?	*[chee soh-noh dehl-leh pahs-seh-djah-teh gwee-dah-teh ?]*	Are there any guided walks?
Avete una guida per le passeggiate locali?	*[ah-veh-teh oo-nah gwee-dah pehr leh pahs-seh-djah-teh loh-cah-lee ?]*	Do you have a guide to local walks?
Conoscete dei bei percorsi?	*[coh-noh-sheh-teh deh-ee beh-ee pehr-cohr-see]*	Do you know any good walks?
Di quanti chilometri è la passeggiata?	*[dee qwahn-tee kee-loh-meh-tree eh lah pahs-seh-djah-tah]*	How many kilometers is the walk?
Quanto tempo ci vuole?	*[qwahn-toh tehm-poh chee voo-oh-leh]*	How long will it take?
È molto ripido?	*[eh mohl-toh ree-pee-doh ?]*	Is it very steep?
Vorremmo fare una scalata.	*[vohr-rehm-moh fah-reh oo-nah scah-lah-tah]*	We'd like to go climbing.

Chapter 26: Telephone, mobile, and text messaging / Telefono e invio di messaggi

Listen to track 57

Vorrei fare una telefonata.	*[vohr-reh-ee fah-reh oo-nah teh-leh-foh-nah-tah]*	I'd like to make a phone call.
C'è un telfono pubblico ?	*[cheh oon teh-leh-foh-noh poob-lee-coh]*	Is there a pay phone?
Una scheda telefonica, per favore.	*[oo-nah skeh-dah teh-leh-foh-nee-cah, pehr fah-voh-reh]*	A phonecard, please.
di ... euro	*[dee ... e-oo-roh]*	for ... euros
Ha un cellulare?	*[hah oon chel-loo-lah-reh]*	Do you have a mobile?
Qual è il suo numero di cellulare?	*[qwal eh eel soo-oh noo-meh-roh dee chel-loo-lah-reh]*	What's your mobile number?
Posso usare il suo cellulare?	*[pohs-soh oo-sah-reh eel soo-oh chel-loo-lah-reh]*	Can I use your mobile?

Il mio numero di cellulare è...	*[eel mee-oh noo-meh-roh dee chel-loo-lah-reh eh]*	My mobile number is...
Pronto?	*[prohn-toh]*	Hello?
Con chi parlo?	*[cohn kee pahr-loh]*	Who's calling?
Sono...	*[soh-noh]*	This is...
Un momento...	*[oon moh-mehn-toh]*	Just a moment...

Listen to track 58

Posso parlare con...?	*[pohs-soh pahr-lah-reh cohn]*	Can I speak to...?
Come ottengo la linea esterna?	*[coh-meh oh-tehn-goh lah lee-neh-ah eh-stehr-nah]*	How do I get an outside line?
Richiamo...	*[ree-kee-ah-moh]*	I'll call back...
...più tardi	*[pyoo tahr-dee]*	...later
...domani	*[doh-mah-nee]*	...tomorrow
glielo/gliela passo. (m/f)	*[lyeh-loh/lyeh-lah pahs-soh]*	I'm putting you through.
Riprovi più tardi, per favore.	*[ree- proh-vee pyoo tahr-dee per fah-voh-reh]*	Please try later.

Vuole lasciare un messaggio?	*[voo-oh-leh lah-shah-reh oon meh-sah-djoh]*	Do you want to leave a message?
Si prega di lasciare un messaggio dopo il segnale acustico.	*[see preh-gah dee lah-sha-reh oon meh-sah-djoh doh-poh eel seh-nyah-leh ah-coos-tee-coh]*	Please leave a message after the tone.
Si prega di spegnere il cellulare.	*[see preh-gah dee speh-nyeh-reh eel chel-loo-lah-reh]*	Please turn your mobile off.
Ti scrivo. / Ti mando un messaggio.	*[tee scree-voh / tee mahn-doh oon meh-sah-djoh]*	I will text you.
Mi puoi mandare un messaggio?	*[mee poo-oh-ee mahn-dah-reh oon meh-sah-djoh]*	Can you text me?

Chapter 27: E-mail

Listen to track 59

Nuovo Messaggio:	*[noo-oh-voh meh-sah-djo]*	New message:
A:	*[ah]*	To:
Da:	*[dah]*	From:
Oggetto:	*[oh-djeh-toh]*	Subject:
CC (copia conoscenza):	*[ko-pee-ah ko-noh-shen-za]*	CC:
CCN (copia conoscenza nascosta):	*[ko-pee-ah ko-noh-shen-za nah-sko-stah]*	BCC:
allegato	*[ahl-leh-gah-toh]*	attachment
invia	*[een-vee-ah]*	send
rispondi	*[rees-pohn-dee]*	reply

Listen to track 60

Ha un indirizzo mail?	*[hah oon een-dee-ree-tso meh-eel]*	Do you have an e-mail address?
Qual è il suo indirizzo mail?	*[qwal eh eel soo-oh een-dee-ree-tso meh-eel]*	What's your e-mail address?
Può fare lo spelling?	*[pwoh fah-reh loh spehl-leeng]*	How do you spell it?

Tutto attaccato.	*[toot-toh ah-tah-cah-toh]*	All in one word.
Tutto minuscolo.	*[toot-toh mee-noos-coh-loh]*	All lower case.
Il mio indirizzo mail...	*[eel mee-oh een-dee-ree-tsoh meh-eel]*	My e-mail address is...
Chiocciola	*[kee-oh-tchoh-lah]*	@
xxpuntoxx-chiocciola... punto it	*[xx poon-toh xx kee-oh-tchoh-lah... poon-toh eet]*	XX.XX@ (company name).it
Posso inviare una mail?	*[pohs-soh een-vee-ah-reh oo-nah meh-eel]*	Can I send an e-mail?
Ha ricevuto la mia mail?	*[hah ree-cheh-voo-toh lah mee-ah meh-eel]*	Did you get my e-mail?

Chapter 28: Computer and internet / Computer ed internet

Listen to track 61

home	*[hom]*	home
username	*[yuu-sehr-neh-eem]*	username
motore di ricerca	*[moh-toh-reh dee ree-chehr-cah]*	search engine
password	*[pahs-sword]*	password
contattaci	*[cohn-tah-tah-chee]*	contact us
torna al menu	*[tohr-nah ahl meh-noo]*	back to menu
indietro	*[een-dee-eh-troh]*	back
Ci sono degli Internet café qui?	*[chee soh-noh deh-lee een-tehr-neht cah-feh qwee]*	Are there any internet cafés here?
Quanto costa connettersi per un'ora?	*[qwahn-toh coh-stah cohn-neh-tehr-see pehr oon oh-rah]*	How much is it to log on for an hour?
Non riesco a connettermi.	*[nohn ree-eh-scoh ah cohn-neh-tehr-mee]*	I can't log on.
accedi	*[ah-tcheh-dee]*	log in
esci	*[eh-shee]*	log out

Chapter 29: Fax

Listen to track 62

A/Da	*[ah/dah]*	To/From
Oggetto	*[oh-djet-toh]*	Re:
Numero di pagine	*[noo-meh-roh dee pah-jee-neh]*	Number of pages
Si prega di trovare in allegato...	*[See prey-gah dee troh-vah-reh een ahl-leh-gah-toh]*	Please find attached...
Avete un fax?	*[ah-veh-teh oon fax]*	Do you have a fax?
Vorrei mandare un fax.	*[vohr-reh-ee mahn-dah-reh oon fax]*	I want to send a fax.
Qual è il suo numero di fax?	*[qwah-leh eel soo-oh noo-meh-roh dee fax]*	What is your fax number?
Il mio numero di fax è...	*[eel mee-oh noo-meh-roh dee fax eh]*	My fax number is...
(non) inviato	*[(nohn) een-veeh-ah-toh]*	(not) sent

Part 5: Talking about mealtimes and eating / Pasti ed alimentazione

One of the best ways to enjoy life is to indulge in food and drink. It is a happy occurrence when you are able to do this while learning a language. Once you have learned some basic Italian vocabulary and phrases related to eating and drinking, you can reward yourself with a trip to an Italian restaurant or café to put these skills to good use. Even better, if you get the chance to go to an Italian speaking country, you will find that this vocabulary comes in very handy.

Chapter 30: At the restaurant / Al ristorante

Listen to track 63

Dove si trova un buon ristorante?	*[doh-veh see troh-vah oon bwon rees-toh-rahn-teh]*	Where is there a good restaurant?
Mi può consigliare...?	*[mee pwoh cohn-see-lyah-reh]*	Can you recommend...?
... un bar	*[oon bahr]*	... a bar
... un café	*[oon cah-feh]*	... a café
... un ristorante	*[oon rees-toh-rahn-teh]*	... a restaurant
Vorrei prenotare un tavolo per ... persone.	*[vohr-reh-ee preh-noh-tah-reh oon tah-voh-loh pehr... pehr-soh-neh]*	I'd like to book a table for ... people.
Per stasera/ domani sera/ per le sette e trenta.	*[pehr stah-seh-rah/doh-mah-nee seh-rah/ pehr leh seht-teh e trehn-tah]*	For tonight/for tomorrow night/ for 7.30.

Listen to track 64

Vorrei ..., per favore.	*[voh-reh-ee ..., pehr fah-voh-reh]*	I'd like ..., please.

un tavolo per (cinque)	*[oon tah-voh-loh pehr (cheen-qweh)]*	a table for (five)
la zona (non) fumatori	*[lah zoh-nah (nohn) foo-mah-toh-ree]*	the (non)smoking section
la lista delle bevande	*[lah lees-tah deh-leh beh-vahn-deh]*	the drink list
la carta dei vini	*[lah cahr-tah deh-ee vee-nee]*	the wine list
il menu	*[eel meh-noo]*	the menu
quel piatto	*[qwel pee-aht-toh]*	that dish
colazione	*[coh-lah-tsyoh-neh]*	breakfast
pranzo	*[prahn-tsoh]*	lunch
cena	*[cheh-nah]*	dinner/supper
un panino	*[oon pah-nee-noh]*	a sandwich
un tramezzino	*[oon trah-meh-tsee-noh]*	a tramezzino sandwich
Uno snack	*[oo-noh snack]*	a snack

Listen to track 65

A che ora viene servita la cena?	*[ah keh oh-rah vee-eh-neh sehr-vee-tah lah cheh-nah]*	At what time is dinner served?

Potremmo pranzare (cenare) adesso?	*[poh-trehm-moh prahn-zah-reh (cheh-nah-reh) ah-dehs-soh]*	Can we have lunch (dinner) now?
la cameriera	*[lah cah-meh-ree-eh-rah]*	the waitress
il cameriere	*[eel cah-meh-ree-eh-reh]*	the waiter
il maître	*[eel meh-tr]*	the headwaiter
Cameriere!	*[cah-meh-ree-eh-reh]*	Waiter!
Scusi?	*[scoo-see]*	Excuse me? (to call waiter/ waitress)
Siamo in due.	*[see-ah-moh een doo-eh]*	There are two of us.
Un tavolo vicino alla finestra, per favore.	*[oon tah-voh-loh vee-chee-noh ahl-lah fee-neh-strah, pehr fah-voh-reh]*	A table near the window, please.
Può portarci il menu, per favore?	*[pwoh pohr-tahr-chee eel meh-noo, pehr fah-voh-reh]*	Can you bring the menu, please?
Per favore, mi può portare il menu?	*[pehr fah-voh-reh, mee pwoh pohr-tah-reh eel meh-noo]*	Please bring me the menu.
Prendo il menu a ... euro, per favore.	*[prehn-doh eel meh-noo ah ... eh-oo-roh, pehr fah-voh-reh]*	I'll have the set menu at ... euros, please.

Listen to track 66

Reading the menu:

Piatto del giorno 7,50 €: pesce o carne o pollo con verdure e patatine fritte

[pee-ah-toh dehl djohr-noh 7,50€: peh-sheh oh cahr-neh oh cohn vehr-doo-reh eh pah-tah-tee-neh freet-teh]

Dish of the day €7.50 - fish or meat or poultry with veg and french fries.

Menu pranzo: antipasto + primo + caffè

[meh-noo prahn-tsoh: ahn-tee-pah-stoh + pree-moh + cah-feh]

Lunchtime menu – starter + main course + coffee.

coperto/ servizio	*[coh-pehr-toh/ sehr-vee-zee-oh]*	cover/service
Cosa consiglia?	*[coh-sah cohn-see-lee-ah]*	What would you recommend?
Può consigliarmi un piatto locale?	*[pwoh cohn-see-lyahr-mee oon pyah-toh loh-cah-leh]*	Can you recommend a local dish?
Qual è il piatto del giorno?	*[qwah-leh eel pyat-toh dehl djohr-noh]*	What is the dish of the day?
Vogliamo cenare alla carta.	*[voh-lee-ah-moh cheh-nah-reh ah lah cahrta]*	We want to dine à la carte.
menu a prezzo fisso	*[meh-noo ah preh-tsoh fees-soh]*	fixed price menu

Listen to track 67

tavolo	*[tah-voh-loh]*	table
una forchetta	*[oo-nah fohr-ket-tah]*	a fork
un coltello	*[oon cohl-tehl-loh]*	a knife
un piatto	*[oon pee-ah-toh]*	a plate
un cucchiaino	*[oon coo-kee-ah-ee-noh]*	a teaspoon
un cucchiaio	*[oon coo-kee-ah-yoh]*	a tablespoon
un cucchiaio	*[oon coo-kee-ah-yoh]*	a spoon
la tazza	*[lah tah-tsah]*	the cup
il bicchiere	*[eel bee-kee-eh-reh]*	the glass
tovagliolo	*[toh-vah-lee-oh-loh]*	napkin
il piatto principale	*[eel pee-ah-toh preen-chee-pah-leh]*	the main course

Listen to track 68

Cosa prende?	*[coh-sah prehn-deh]*	What will you have?
Vorrei qualcosa di semplice.	*[voh-reh-ee quahl-coh-sah dee sehm-plee-cheh]*	I would like something simple.
Non troppo piccante.	*[nohn trohp-poh pee-cahn-teh]*	Not too spicy.

Mi piace la carne al sangue.	*[mee pee-ah-cheh la cahr-neh ahl sahn-gweh]*	I like the meat rare.
ben cotta	*[behn coht-tah]*	well done
Da portare via, per favore.	*[dah pohr-tah-reh vee-ah, pehr fah-voh-reh]*	Take it away, please.
Questo è freddo.	*[qwes-toh eh freh-doh]*	This is cold.
Non ho ordinato questo.	*[nohn hoh ohr-dee-nah-toh qweh-stoh]*	I did not order this.
Posso cambiarlo con un'insalata?	*[pohs-soh cahm-bee-ahr-loh cohn oon een-sah-lah-tah]*	May I change this for a salad?
Il conto, per favore.	*[eel cohn-toh, pehr fah-voh-reh]*	The check, please.
il conto	*[eel cohn-toh]*	the bill
lo scontrino	*[loh scohn-tree-noh]*	the receipt

Listen to track 69

Posso avere il conto, per favore?	*[poh-soh ah-veh-reh eel cohn-toh, pehr fah-voh-reh]*	Could I have the bill, please?

Il coperto è incluso?	*[eel coh-pehr-toh eh een-cloo-soh]*	Is the service charge included?
C'è un errore nel conto.	*[cheh oon ehr-roh-reh nehl cohn-toh]*	There is a mistake in the bill.
Questi addebiti a cosa si riferiscono?	*[qweh-stee ah-deh-bee-tee ah coh-sah see ree-feh-rees-coh-noh]*	What are these charges for?
Tenga il resto.	*[tehn-gah eel reh-stoh]*	Keep the change.
Il cibo e il servizio sono stati ottimi.	*[eel chee-boh eh eel sehr-vee-tsee-oh soh-noh stah-tee oh-tee-mee]*	The food and service were excellent.
acqua potabile	*[ah-qwah poh-tah-bee-leh]*	drinking water
con ghiaccio	*[cohn gyee-ah-tchoh]*	with ice
senza ghiaccio	*[sehn-tsah gyee-ah-tchoh]*	without ice
antipasto	*[ahn-tee-pah-stoh]*	starter
il dolce	*[eel dohl-cheh]*	the dessert

Listen to track 70

il pesce	*[eel peh-sheh]*	the fish
la carne	*[lah cahr-neh]*	the meat
l'insalata	*[leen-sah-lah-tah]*	the salad

la zuppa	[la zoop-pah]	the soup
pepe	[peh-peh]	pepper
sale	[sah-leh]	salt
zucchero	[zoo-ke-roh]	sugar
freddo/fredda (m/f)	[freh-doh/freh-dah]	cold
caldo/calda (m/f)	[cahl-doh/cahl-dah]	hot
un altro ..., per favore.	[oon ahl-troh ..., pehr fah-voh-reh]	Another ..., please.
Qual è la specialità locale?	[qwahl-eh lah speh-cha-lee-tah loh-cah-leh]	What's the local speciality?
Qual è il piatto della casa?	[qwahl-eh eel pyah-toh dehl-lah cah-sah]	What's the house speciality?

Listen to track 71

Cos'è quello?	[coh-seh qwel-loh]	What's that?
Posso ...?	[pohs-soh]	Can I ...?
fumare	[foo-mah-reh]	smoke
affamato/ affamata (m/f)	[ah-fah-mah-toh/ah-fah-mah-tah]	hungry
assetato/ assetata (m/f)	[ah-seh-tah-toh/ah-seh-tah-tah]	thirsty
Buon appetito!	[bwon ah-peh-tee-toh]	Enjoy your meal!

Cosa c'è dentro?	*[coh-sah cheh dehn-troh]*	What is in this?
Prendo questo.	*[prehn-doh qweh-stoh]*	I'll have this.
Dell'altro pane, per favore.	*[dehl-lahl-troh pah-neh, pehr fah-voh-reh]*	More bread, please.
Dell'altra acqua, per favore.	*[dehl-lahl-trah ah-qwah, pehr fah-voh-reh]*	More water, please.
Il pasto era delizioso.	*[eel pahs-toh eh-rah deh-lee-tsyoh-soh]*	The meal was delicious.
Il conto, per favore.	*[eel cohn-toh, pehr fah-voh-reh]*	The bill, please.
Il servizio è incluso?	*[eel sehr-vee-tsyoh eh een-cloo-soh]*	Is service included?

Chapter 31: Foods / Il cibo

Listen to track 72

il pane	*[eel pah-neh]*	the bread
il burro	*[eel boor-roh]*	the butter
lo zucchero	*[loh zook-keh-roh]*	the sugar
il sale	*[eel sah-leh]*	the salt
il pepe	*[eel peh-peh]*	the pepper
la salsa	*[lah sahl-sah]*	the sauce
l'olio	*[loh-leeh-oh]*	the oil
l'aceto	*[lah-cheh-toh]*	the vinegar
la mostarda/la senape	*[lah mohs-tahr-dah/lah sehn-ah-peh]*	the mustard
l'aglio	*[lah-lee-oh]*	the garlic

Listen to track 73

del pollo arrosto	*[dehl pohl-loh ah-roh-stoh]*	some roast chicken
del pollo fritto	*[dehl pohl-loh freet-toh]*	some fried chicken
manzo	*[mahn-zoh]*	beef
agnello	*[ah-nee-yel-loh]*	lamb
fegato	*[feh-gah-toh]*	liver
maiale	*[mah-yah-leh]*	pork
arrosto di manzo	*[ahr-roh-stoh dee mahn-zoh]*	roast beef
bistecca	*[bees-tek-cah]*	steak

| salsicce | *[sahl-see-tcheh]* | sausages |
| vitello | *[vee-tehl-loh]* | veal |

Listen to track 74

orata	*[oh-rah-tah]*	sea bream
spigola	*[spee-goh-lah]*	sea bass
calamaro	*[cah-lah-mah-roh]*	squid
aragosta	*[ah-rah-goh-stah]*	lobster
sardine	*[sahr-dee-neh]*	sardines
gamberi	*[gahm-beh-ree]*	shrimps
polpo	*[pohl-poh]*	octopus
cozze	*[coh-tseh]*	mussels

Listen to track 75

bruschetta	*[broos-ket-tah]*	(toasted bread topped with fresh diced tomatoes, garlic, basil, olive oil, and salt)
tagliere di affettati	*[tah-lee-eh-reh dee ah-feht-tah-tee]*	(assortment of cured meats)
Insalata Caprese	*[een-sah-lah-tah cah-preh-seh]*	(fresh slices of tomatoes, mozzarella, basil, olive oil, and salt)
grigliata di verdure	*[gree-lyah-tah dee vehr-doo-reh]*	(grilled mixed vegetables)

Pizza Margherita	*[pee-tsah mahr-gwe-ree-tah]*	(Tomato, mozzarella, olive oil and basil)
Rigatoni alla Amatriciana	*[ree-gah-toh-nee ahl-lah-mah-tree-chah-nah]*	(pasta with tomato sauce, pork cheek, and pepper)
Rigatoni alla Carbonara	*[ree-gah-toh-nee ahl-lah cahr-boh-nah-rah]*	(pasta with pork cheek, creamy egg and pecorino cheese, and pepper)
Spaghetti Cacio e Pepe	*[spah-gweh-tee cah-tcho eh peh-peh]*	(pasta with creamy pecorino cheese and pepper)
Tonnarelli alla Gricia	*[tohn-nah-rehl-lee ahl-lah gree-cah]*	(long pasta with pork cheek, creamy pecorino cheese, and pepper)
Tiramisù	*[tee-rah-mee-soo]*	(dessert with layers of Savoiardi, mascarpone cream, espresso, liqueur, and cocoa)

Chapter 32: Breakfast foods / La colazione

<u>Listen to track 76</u>

Posso avere del succo di frutta, per favore?	*[poh-tsoh ah-veh-reh dehl sooc-coh dee froot-tah, pehr fah-voh-reh]*	May I have some fruit juice?
spremuta d'arancia	*[spreh-moo-tah dah-rahn-cha]*	orange juice
prugne cotte	*[proo-nee-eh coh-teh]*	stewed prunes
succo di pomodoro	*[sooc-coh dee poh-moh-doh-roh]*	tomato juice
marmellata	*[mahr-mehl-lah-tah]*	marmalade
toast con la marmellata	*[tohs-t cohn lah mahr-mehl-lah-tah]*	toast and jam
panini	*[pah-nee-nee]*	rolls
una frittata	*[oo-nah free-tah-tah]*	an omelet

<u>Listen to track 77</u>

uova	*[woh-vah]*	eggs
uova alla coque	*[woh-vah ahl-lah kok]*	soft-boiled eggs
uova sode cottura media	*[woh-vah soh-deh coht-too-rah meh-dee-ah]*	medium boiled eggs

uova sode ben cotte	*[woh-vah soh-deh behn coht-teh]*	hard-boiled eggs
uova al tegamino	*[woh-vah ahl teh-gah-mee-noh]*	fried egg
uova strapazzate	*[woh-vah strah-pah-tsah-teh]*	scrambled eggs
uova e pancetta	*[woh-vah eh pahn-tchet-tah]*	bacon and eggs
uova e prosciutto	*[woh-vah eh proh-shoot-toh]*	ham and eggs

Listen to track 78

cappuccino	*[cahp-poot-chee-noh]*	cappuccino
latte	*[laht-teh]*	milk
caffé	*[cah-feh]*	coffee
tè	*[teh]*	tea
camomilla	*[cah-moh-meel-lah]*	chamomile
latte macchiato	*[laht-teh mah-kee-ah-toh]*	milk with coffee
caffelatte	*[cah-feh-laht-teh]*	white coffee
caffé lungo	*[cah-feh loon-goh]*	large coffee

Listen to track 79

cornetto	*[cohr-net-toh]*	croissant
biscotti	*[bee-scott-tee]*	cookies
fette biscottate	*[feh-teh bees-coh-tah-teh]*	rusks
avena	*[ah-veh-nah]*	oats
frutta	*[froot-tah]*	fruits
burro	*[boor-roh]*	butter
miele	*[mee-eh-leh]*	honey
cioccolata calda	*[choc-coh-lah-tah cahl-dah]*	hot chocolate
frullato	*[froo-lah-toh]*	shake
frappé	*[frah-peh]*	milk shake
torta	*[tohr-tah]*	cake
una fetta di torta	*[oo-nah feht-tah dee tohr-tah]*	a slice of cake

Chapter 33: Special diets & allergies / Dieta e allergie

Listen to track 80

C'è un ristorante vegetariano qui vicino?	*[cheh oon rees-toh-rahn-teh veh-djeh-tah-ree-ah-noh qwee vee-chee-noh]*	Is there a vegetarian restaurant near here?
Avete dei piatti vegetariani?	*[ah-veh-teh deh-ee pyat-tee veh-djeh-tah-ree-ah-nee]*	Do you have vegetarian food?
Quali sono i piatti senza carne/pesce?	*[qwah-lee soh-noh ee pyat-tee sehn-tsah cahr-neh/peh-sheh]*	Which dishes have no meat/ fish?
Non mi piace la carne.	*[nohn mee pee-ah-cheh lah cahr-neh]*	I don't like meat.
Vorrei la pasta come primo piatto.	*[voh-reh-ee lah pah-stah coh-meh pree-moh pee-aht-toh]*	I'd like pasta as a main course.
È fatto con brodo vegetale?	*[eh faht-toh cohn broh-doh veh-djeh-tah-leh]*	Is it made with vegetable stock?
Potrebbe preparare un/ uno/una .... senza...?	*[poh-treh-beh preh-pah-rah-reh oon/oo-noh/oo-nah... sehn-tsah]*	Could you prepare a ... without...?

brodo di carne	*[broh-doh dee cahr-neh]*	meat stock
Sono allergico/ allergica... (m/f)	*[soh-noh ahl-lehr-jee-coh/ ahl-lehr-jee-cah]*	I'm allergic...
...ai latticini	*[ah-ee laht-tee-chee-nee]*	...to dairy products
...al glutine	*[ahl gloo-tee-neh]*	...to gluten
...al glutammato	*[ahl gloo-tah-mah-toh]*	...to MSG
...alla frutta secca	*[ahl-lah froot-tah seh-cah]*	...to nuts
...ai frutti di mare	*[ah-ee froot-tee dee mah-reh]*	...to seafood
...sedano	*[seh-dah-noh]*	...celery

Chapter 34: Appetizer, soups, and entrées / Antipasti, zuppe, primi piatti

Listen to track 81

antipasto	*[ahn-tee-pah-stoh]*	appetizer
antipasto di mare	*[ahn-tee-pah-stoh dee mah-reh]*	seafood appetizer
salumi	*[sah-loo-mee]*	cured meat
formaggi	*[fohr-mah-djee]*	cheeses
noccioline	*[noh-tcho-lee-neh]*	peanuts
patatine	*[pah-tah-tee-neh]*	chips
Vorrei una zuppa di pollo.	*[voh-reh-ee oo-nah zoop-pah dee pohl-loh]*	I'd like some chicken soup.
minestrone	*[mee-neh-stroh-neh]*	vegetable soup
zuppa di legumi	*[zoop-pah dee leh-goo-mee]*	legumes soup
lenticchie	*[lehn-tee-kee-eh]*	lentils
ceci	*[che-tchee]*	chickpeas
fagioli	*[fah-djoh-lee]*	beans

Listen to track 82

riso	*[ree-soh]*	rice
farro	*[fahr-roh]*	spelt (a type of wheat grain)

ravioli	*[rah-vee-oh-lee]*	Italian dumplings
pasta con...	*[pah-stah cohn]*	pasta with...
...sugo	*[soo-goh]*	...tomato sauce
...pesto	*[peh-stoh]*	...pesto
...ragù alla bolognese	*[rah-goo ahl-lah boh-loh-nee-eh-seh]*	...bolognese sauce
... in bianco	*[... een bee-ahn-coh]*	... butter or oil
lasagna	*[lah-sah-nyah]*	lasagna
pasta al forno	*[pah-stah ahl fohr-noh]*	baked pasta

Chapter 35: Vegetables and salad / Verdure e insalata

Listen to track 83

Vorrei degli asparagi.	*[voh-reh-ee deh-lee ah-spah-rah-djee]*	I would like some asparagus.
carote	*[cah-roh-teh]*	carrots
cavolo	*[cah-voh-loh]*	cabbage
cavolfiore	*[cah-vohl-fyoh-reh]*	cauliflower
sedano	*[seh-dah-noh]*	celery
olive	*[oh-lee-veh]*	olives
prezzemolo	*[preh-tseh-moh-loh]*	parsley
origano	*[oh-ree-gah-noh]*	oregano
alloro	*[ahl-loh-roh]*	bay leaf
cetriolo	*[che-tree-oh-loh]*	cucumber
menta	*[mehn-tah]*	mint
basilico	*[bah-see-lee-coh]*	basil

Listen to track 84

insalata	*[een-sah-lah-tah]*	salad
lattuga	*[lah-too-gah]*	lettuce
valeriana	*[vah-leh-ryah-nah]*	valerian
rucola	*[roo-coh-lah]*	arugula/rocket

funghi	*[foon-gyee]*	mushrooms
cipolle	*[chee-poll-leh]*	onions
piselli	*[pee-seh-lee]*	peas
peperoni	*[peh-peh-roh-nee]*	peppers
spinaci	*[spee-nah-chee]*	spinach
patate	*[pah-tah-teh]*	potatoes
patate lesse	*[pah-tah-teh lehs-seh]*	boiled potatoes
patatine fritte	*[pah-tah-tee-neh freet-teh]*	fried potatoes
puré di patate	*[poo-reh dee pah-tah-teh]*	mashed potatoes

Listen to track 85

pomodori	*[poh-moh-doh-ree]*	tomatoes
zucca	*[zooc-cah]*	pumpkin
melanzane	*[meh-lahn-tsah-neh]*	eggplant
zucchine	*[zoo-kee-neh]*	zucchini
aglio	*[ah-lee-oh]*	garlic
rosmarino	*[rohs-mah-ree-noh]*	rosemary
carciofi	*[cahr-tchoh-fee]*	artichoks
rapa	*[rah-pah]*	turnip
cicoria	*[chee-coh-ree-ah]*	chicory
bietola	*[bee-eh-toh-lah]*	chard
cardo	*[cahr-doh]*	cardoon (artichoke thistle)

Chapter 36: Fruits / Frutta

Listen to track 86

Vorrei una mela.	*[voh-reh-ee oo-nah meh-lah]*	I would like an apple.
pera	*[peh-rah]*	pear
delle ciliegie	*[dehl-leh chee-lee-eh-djeh]*	some cherries
un pompelmo	*[oon pawn-pehl-moh]*	a grapefruit
un'arancia	*[oon ah-rahn-tcha]*	an orange
dell'uva	*[dehl oo-vah]*	some grapes
limone	*[lee-moh-neh]*	lemon
melone	*[meh-loh-neh]*	melon
anguria	*[ahn-goo-ryah]*	watermelon
pesca	*[peh-scah]*	peach
lamponi	*[lahm-poh-nee]*	raspberries
fragole	*[frah-goh-leh]*	strawberries
more	*[moh-reh]*	blackberries
ribes	*[ree-bes]*	currant
albicocca	*[ahl-bee-cohc-cah]*	apricot
ananas	*[ah-nah-nahs]*	pineapple
banana	*[bah-nah-nah]*	banana
kiwi	*[kee-wee]*	kiwi
mandarino	*[mahn-dah-ree-noh]*	tangerine

Chapter 37: Desserts / I dolci

Listen to track 87

Potrei avere un po' di torta?	*[poh-treh-ee ah-veh-reh oon poh dee tohr-tah]*	May I have some cake?
...del formaggio	*[dehl fohr-mah-djoh]*	...some cheese
...dei biscotti	*[deh-ee bee-scott-tee]*	...some cookies
...delle crêpes	*[dehl-leh creh-pp]*	...some crêpes
...della crema pasticcera	*[dehl-lah creh-mah pah-stee-tcheh-rah]*	...some custard
...gelato	*[djeh-lah-toh]*	...ice cream
...del gelato al cioccolato	*[dehl djeh-lah-toh ahl tchoh-coh-lah-toh]*	...some chocolate ice cream

Chapter 38: Beverages & drinks / Bevande

Listen to track 88

un drink	[oon drink]	a drink
un succo di frutta	[oon soo-coh dee froot-tah]	a fruit drink
una bibita	[oo-nah bee-bee-tah]	a soft drink
una bottiglia di acqua minerale	[oo-nah boh-tee-lya dee ah-qwah mee-neh-rah-leh]	a bottle of mineral water
acqua	[ac-qwah]	water
acqua minerale	[ac-qwah mee-neh-rah-leh]	mineral water
acqua frizzante	[ac-qwah free-tsahn-teh]	sparkling mineral water
latte	[laht-teh]	milk
tè	[teh]	tea
vino	[vee-noh]	wine
birra	[beer-rah]	beer
succo d'arancia	[sooc-coh dah-rahn-tcha]	orange juice
spremuta d'arancia	[spreh-moo-tah dah-rahn-tcha]	fresh orange juice

Listen to track 89

limonata	[lee-moh-nah-tah]	lemonade

analcolico	*[ahn-ahl-coh-lee-coh]*	soft drink
un'aranciata	*[oon ah-rahn-cha-tah]*	an orangeade
con limone	*[cohn lee-moh-neh]*	with lemon
frizzante	*[free-tsahn-teh]*	fizzy
calda	*[cahl-dah]*	hot
freddo	*[freh-doh]*	cold
a temperatura ambiente	*[ah tehm-peh-rah-too-rah ahm-bee-ehn-teh]*	at room temperature
effervescente	*[eh-fehr-veh-shehn-teh]*	sparkling
liscia	*[lee-sha]*	still

Chapter 39: Café / Caffetteria

Listen to track 90

un caffé	*[oon cah-feh]*	a coffee
caffé lungo	*[cah-feh loon-goh]*	black coffee
caffé	*[cah-feh]*	espresso
un caffé...	*[oon cah-feh]*	(cup of) coffee...
un caffé macchiato caldo	*[oon cah-feh mah-kyah-toh cahl-doh]*	coffee with hot milk
un caffé macchiato freddo	*[oon cah-feh mah-kyah-toh freh-doh]*	coffee with cold milk
caffé con panna	*[cah-feh cohn pahn-nah]*	coffee with cream
caffé con panna montata	*[cah-feh cohn pahn-nah mohn-tah-tah]*	coffee with whipped cream
decaffeinato	*[deh-cah-feh-ee-nah-toh]*	decaffeinated
caffelatte	*[cah-feh-laht-teh]*	white coffee
caffelatte con schiuma	*[cah-feh-lah-teh cohn skee-oo-mah]*	white creamy coffee
caffelatte con schiuma in tazza grande	*[cah-feh-lah-teh cohn skee-oo-mah een tah-tsah grahn-deh]*	large white creamy coffee

Listen to track 91

caffé freddo	*[cah-feh frehd-doh]*	iced coffee
caffé solubile	*[cah-feh soh-loo-bee-leh]*	instant coffee
del latte	*[dehl laht-teh]*	some milk
del tè	*[dehl teh]*	some tea
un tè	*[oon teh]*	a (cup of) tea ...
tè con latte	*[teh cohn laht-teh]*	tea with milk
infuso	*[een-foo-soh]*	herb tea
tè alla menta	*[teh ahl-lah mehn-tah]*	mint tea
tè al limone	*[teh ahl lee-moh-neh]*	lemon tea
zucchero	*[zooc-keh-roh]*	sugar
senza zucchero	*[sehn-tsah zooc-keh-roh]*	without sugar
calda	*[cahl-dah]*	hot
freddo	*[freh-doh]*	cold

Chapter 40: In a bar / Al bar

Listen to track 92

digestivo	*[dee-jess-tee-voh]*	liqueur
alcool	*[ahl-coh-ohl]*	alcohol
il barman	*[eel bahr-mahn]*	The bartender
Quali liquori avete?	*[qwah-lee lee-qwoh-ree ah-veh-teh]*	What liqueurs do you have?
La carta dei vini, per favore.	*[lah cahr-tah deh-ee vee-nee, pehr fah-voh-reh]*	The wine list, please.
carta dei vini	*[cahr-tah deh-ee vee-nee]*	wine list
vino	*[vee-noh]*	wine
vino rosso	*[vee-noh ross-oh]*	red wine
vino bianco	*[vee-noh bee-ahn-coh]*	white wine

Listen to track 93

Una bottiglia..	*[oo-nah boh-tee-lyah]*	A bottle...
Una caraffa	*[oo-nah cah-rahf-fah]*	A carafe...
...del vino della casa	*[dehl vee-noh dehl-lah cah-sah]*	...of the house wine

...vino locale	*[vee-noh loh-ca-leh]*	...regional wine
...rosé	*[raw-zey]*	...rosé
...della Birra (chiara, scura)	*[dehl-lah beer-rah (kee-ah-rah, scoo-rah]*	...some beer (light, dark)
...birra alla spina	*[beer-rah ahl-lah spee-nah]*	...draught beer
...birra scura	*[beer-rah scoo-rah]*	... dark beer
...birra rossa	*[beer-rah rohs-sah]*	...fairly dark beer
...secco/brut	*[seh-koh/ broot]*	...very dry
...gin	*[geen]*	...gin

Listen to track 94

Un bicchiere di Negramaro	*[oon bee-kee-eh-reh dee neh-grah-mah-roh]*	A glass of Negramaro
per due	*[pehr doo-eh]*	for two
per me	*[pehr meh]*	for me
per lui/lei	*[pehr loo-ee/ leh-ee]*	for him/her
per noi	*[pehr noh-ee]*	for us
con ghiaccio, per favore	*[cohn gwee-ah-tcho, pehr fah-voh-reh]*	with ice, please
ghiaccio	*[gwee-at-choh]*	ice

cubetto di ghiaccio	*[coo-bet-toh dee gwee-at-choh]*	ice cube
Prendiamone un altro.	*[prehn-dee-ah-moh-neh oon ahl-troh]*	Let's have another.
Salute! / Cin Cin!	*[sah-loo-teh]* / *[cheen cheen]*	To your health!

Part 6: Traveling & planning (trips, weather, activities) / Viaggi e pianificazione (meteo e attività)

Learning Italian often inspires you to daydream about traveling and planning trips to Italian-speaking countries. This type of wanderlust can be greatly expedited with some Italian vocabulary and phrases related to traveling and planning. From the beach to the mountains, from camping to sightseeing, this chapter will give you some practical and useful hints for planning your dream holiday.

Chapter 41: A place to stay / Posti do soggiornare

Listen to track 95

un hotel economico	*[oon hotel eh-coh-noh-mee-coh]*	an inexpensive hotel
Sto cercando un buon hotel.	*[stoh chehr-chan-doh oon boo-ohn hotel]*	I am looking for a good hotel.
una pensione	*[oo-nah pen-see-oh-neh]*	a boarding house
appartamento completamente arredato	*[ahp-pahr-tah-mehn-toh cohm-pleh-tah-mehn-teh ah-reh-dah-toh]*	fully furnished apartment
(non) Voglio stare in centro.	*[(nohn) voh-lee-oh stah-reh een chen-troh]*	I (do not) want to be in the center of town.
dove non c'è rumore	*[doh-veh nohn cheh roo-moh-reh]*	where it is not noisy
Vorrei prenotare una stanza, per favore.	*[voh-reh-ee preh-noh-tah-reh oo-nah stahn-tsah, pehr fah-voh-reh]*	I'd like to book a room, please.
Ho una prenotazione per oggi.	*[hoh oo-nah preh-noh-tah-tsyoh-neh pehr odd-djee]*	I have a reservation for today.
Il mio nome è...	*[eel mee-oh noh-meh eh]*	My name is...

Listen to track 96

Avete una stanza/un posto libero?	*[ah-veh-teh oo-nah stahn-tsah/oon poh-stoh lee-beh-roh]*	Do you have a room/a vacancy?
una stanza con aria condizionata	*[oo-nah stahn-tsah cohn ah-ree-ah cohn-dee-tsyoh-nah-tah]*	an air conditioned room
una singola	*[oo-nah seen-goh-lah]*	a single room
una doppia	*[oo-nah doh-pyah]*	a double room
una doppia	*[oo-nah doh-pyah]*	a twin room
senza pasti/ senza vitto	*[sehn-tsah pah-stee/sehn-tsah veet-toh]*	without meals
con un letto matrimoniale	*[cohn oon leht-toh mah-tree-moh-nee-ah-leh]*	with a double bed
con bagno	*[cohn bah-nee-oh]*	with a bathroom
con doccia	*[cohn-doh-tchah]*	with a shower
con due letti singoli	*[cohn doo-eh leht-tee seen-goh-lee]*	with twin beds
una suite	*[oo-nah sweet]*	a suite
per questa notte	*[pehr qweh-stah not-teh]*	for tonight

Listen to track 97

Vorrei restare per (due) notti.	*[vohr-reh-ee reh-stah-reh pehr (doo-eh) not-tee]*	I'd like to stay for (two) nights.
per tre giorni	*[pehr treh djohr-nee]*	for three days
per due persone	*[pehr doo-eh pehr-soh-neh]*	for two
Qual è il costo a notte?	*[qwah-leh eel coh-stoh ah not-teh]*	What is the rate per day?
Quanto costa a...?	*[qwahn-toh coh-stah ah]*	How much is it per...?
...notte	*[not-teh]*	...night
...persona	*[pehr-soh-nah]*	...person
Tasse e servizio in camera sono inclusi?	*[tahs-seh eh sehr-vee-tsyoh een cah-meh-rah soh-noh een-cloo-see]*	Are tax and room service included?
Vorrei vedere la stanza.	*[vohr-reh-ee veh-deh-reh lah stahn-tsah]*	I would like to see the room.
Non mi piace questa.	*[nohn mee pyah-tcheh qweh-stah]*	I do not like this one.

Listen to track 98

al piano di sopra	*[ahl pyah-noh dee soh-prah]*	upstairs
al piano di sotto	*[ahl pyah-noh dee soht-toh]*	downstairs

C'è l'ascensore?	*[cheh lah-shehn-soh-reh]*	Is there an elevator?
una cassaforte	*[oo-nah cahs-sah-fohr-teh]*	a safe
Il servizio in camera, per favore.	*[eel sehr-vee-tsyoh een cah-meh-rah, pehr fah-voh-reh]*	Room service, please.
Per favore, può mandare un facchino nella mia stanza?	*[pehr fah-voh-reh, pwoh mahn-dah-reh oon fah-kee-noh nehl-lah mee-ah stahn-tsah]*	Please send a porter to my room.
una cameriera	*[oo-nah cah-meh-ryeh-rah]*	a chambermaid
un fattorino	*[oon faht-toh-ree-noh]*	a bellhop
Per favore, mi chiami alle 9.	*[pehr fah-voh-reh, mee kee-ah-mee ahl-leh noh-veh]*	Please call me at nine o'clock.
Vorrei la colazione in stanza.	*[voh-reh-ee lah coh-lah-tsyoh-neh een stahn-tsah]*	I would like breakfast in my room.
Torni più tardi.	*[tohr-nee pyoo tahr-dee]*	Come back later.

Listen to track 99

Può portarmi un'altra coperta?	*[pwoh pohr-tahr-mee oon ahl-trah coh-pehr-tah]*	Could you bring me another blanket?

Potrei avere un'altra (coperta)?	[poh-treh-ee ah-veh-reh oon ahl-trah (coh-pehr-tah)]	Can I get another (blanket)?
un cuscino	[oon coo-shee-noh]	a pillow
una federa	[oo-nah feh-deh-rah]	a pillowcase
lenzuolo	[lehn-tswoh-loh]	sheet
appendiabiti	[ah-pehn-dee-ah-bee-tee]	hangers
sapone	[sah-poh-neh]	soap
asciugamani	[ah-shoo-gah-mah-nee]	towels
un tappetino per il bagno	[oon tah-peh-tee-noh pehr eel bah-nyoh]	a bath mat
la vasca da bagno	[lah vahs-cah dah bah-nyoh]	the bathtub
il lavabo	[eel lah-vah-boh]	the sink
la carta igienica	[lah cahr-tah ee-djeh-nee-cah]	toilet paper

Listen to track 100

Vorrei parlare con il direttore.	[vohr-reh-ee pahr-lah-reh cohn eel dee-reht-toh-reh]	I would like to speak to the manager.
La mia chiave, per favore.	[lah mee-ah kee-ah-veh, pehr fah-voh-reh]	My room key, please.

Potrei avere la mia chiave, per favore?	*[pot-reh-ee ah-veh-reh lah mee-ah kee-ah-veh, pehr fah-voh-reh]*	Could I have my key, please?
Ci sono lettere o messaggi per me?	*[chee soh-noh leht-teh-reh oh mess-sah-djee pehr meh]*	Do I have any letters or messages?
Qual è il numero della mia stanza?	*[qwah-leh eel noo-meh-roh dehl-lah mee-ah stahn-tsah]*	What is my room number?
Vado via alle 10.	*[vah-doh vee-ah ahl-leh dee-eh-tchee]*	I am leaving at ten o'clock
Per favore, mi faccia il conto.	*[pehr fah-voh-reh, mee fah-tcha eel cohn-toh]*	Please make out my bill.
Accetta un assegno?	*[ah-tcheh-tah oon ahs-seh-nyoh]*	Will you accept a check?
Posso pagare con la carta di credito?	*[pohs-soh pah-gah-reh cohn lah cahr-tah dee creh-dee-toh]*	Can I pay by credit card?
Per favore, può inviare la mia lettera a...	*[pehr fah-voh-reh, pwoh een-vee-ah-reh lah mee-ah let-teh-rah ah]*	Please forward my mail to...

Posso lasciare i bagagli qui fino a domani?	*[pohs-soh lah-shah-reh ee bah-gal-lee qwee fee-noh ah doh-mah-nee]*	May I store baggage here until tomorrow?

Listen to track 101

Dov'è un...?	*[doh-veh oon]*	Where's a...?
...campeggio	*[.cahm-peh-djoh]*	...camping ground
...ostello	*[oh-stehl-loh]*	...youth hostel
Può consigliarmi un posto...?	*[pwoh cohn-see-lee-ahr-mee oon poh-stoh]*	Can you recommend somewhere...?
...economico	*[eh-coh-noh-mee-coh]*	...cheap
...buono	*[bwoh-noh]*	...good
...vicino	*[vee-chee-noh]*	...nearby
Posso campeggiare qui?	*[pohs-soh cahm-peh-djah-reh qwee]*	Am I allowed to camp here?
Dov'è il campeggio più vicino?	*[doh-veh eel cahm-peh-djoh pyoo vee-chee-noh]*	Where's the nearest campsite?
A che ora viene servita la colazione?	*[ah keh oh-rah vyeh-neh sehr-vee-tah lah coh-lah-tsyoh-neh]*	When/Where is breakfast served?

115

| Per favore, mi svegli alle (sette). | *[pehr fah-voh-reh, mee sveh-lee ahl-leh (seht-teh)]* | Please wake me at (seven). |

Listen to track 102

La stanza è...	*[lah stahn-tsah eh]*	The room is too...
...costosa	*[coh-stoh-sah]*	...expensive
...rumorosa	*[roo-moh-roh-sah]*	...noisy
...piccola	*[pee-coh-lah]*	...small
...non funziona	*[nohn foon-tsyoh-nah]*	...doesn't work.
l'aria condizionata	*[lah-ree-ah cohn-dee-tsyoh-nah-tah]*	the air conditioning
il ventilatore	*[eel vehn-tee-lah-toh-reh]*	fan
Il bagno non è pulito.	*[eel bah-nee-oh nohn eh poo-lee-toh]*	The toilet isn't clean.
A che ora è il checkout?	*[ah keh oh-rah eh eel checkout]*	What time is checkout?
Per favore, posso avere...?	*[pehr fah-voh-reh, pohs-soh ah-veh-reh]*	Could I have my..., please?
la mia cauzione	*[lah mee-ah cah-oo-tsyoh-neh]*	deposit

passaporto	*[pahs-sah-pohr-toh]*	passport
i miei valori	*[ee mee-eh-ee vah-loh-ree]*	valuables

Chapter 42: The weather / Il meteo

Listen to track 103

Che tempo fa?	*[keh tehm-poh fah]*	What's the weather like?
È nuovoloso.	*[eh noo-voh-loh-soh]*	It's cloudy.
Fa freddo.	*[fah freh-doh]*	It's cold.
Fa caldo.	*[fah cahl-doh]*	It's hot.
Fa caldo.	*[fah cahl-doh]*	It's warm
Sta piovendo.	*[stah pyoh-vehn-doh]*	It's raining.
Sta nevicando.	*[stah neh-vee-cahn-doh]*	It's snowing.
È soleggiato.	*[eh soh-leh-djah-toh]*	It's sunny.
C'è vento.	*[cheh vehn-toh]*	It's windy.
C'è nebbia.	*[cheh neh-byah]*	It's foggy.

Chapter 43: Amusements / Divertimenti

Listen to track 104

Vorrei andare a un concerto.	*[voh-reh-ee ahn-dah-reh ah oon cohn-chehr-toh]*	I would like to go to a concert.
Vorrei andare...	*[voh-reh-ee ahn-dah-reh]*	I feel like going ...
...al cinema	*[ahl chee-neh-mah]*	...to the movies
...in discoteca	*[een dee-sko-teh-kah]*	...to a night club
...all'opera	*[ahl oh-peh-rah]*	...to the opera
...all'ufficio prenotazioni	*[ahl oof-fee-choh preh-noh-tah-tsyoh-nee]*	...to the booking office
...a teatro	*[ah teh-ah-troh]*	...to the theater
...al ristorante	*[ahl rees-toh-rahn-teh]*	...to the restaurant
A che ora inizia lo spettacolo serale/il prossimo spettacolo?	*[ah keh oh-rah ee-nee-tsyah loh speh-tah-coh-loh seh-rah-leh/ eel proh-see-moh speh-tah-coh-loh]*	When does the evening performance/the next show start?

Listen to track 105

Ci sono posti per questa sera?	*[chee soh-noh poh-stee pehr qweh-stah seh-rah]*	Have you any seats for tonight?
un posto prenotato/ riservato	*[oon poh-stoh preh-noh-tah-toh/ree-sehr-vah-toh]*	a reserved seat
sulla balconata	*[sool-lah bahl-coh-nah-tah]*	in the balcony
Si vede bene da lì?	*[see veh-deh beh-neh dah-lee]*	Can I see well from there?
Dove possiamo andare a ballare?	*[doh-veh pohs-see-ah-moh ahn-dah-reh ah bahl-lah-reh]*	Where can we go to dance?
Mi concede questo ballo?	*[mee cohn-cheh-deh qweh-stoh bahl-loh]*	May I have this dance?
Dove posso trovare...?	*[doh-veh pohs-soh troh-vah-reh]*	Where can I find...?
...discoteche	*[dee-skoh-teh-keh]*	...clubs
...locali gay	*[loh-cah-lee gay]*	...gay venues
...pub	*[pub]*	...pubs

Listen to track 106

Ti piace...?	*[tee pyah-cheh]*	Do you like...?
Mi piace...	*[mee pyah-cheh]*	I like...
Non mi piace...	*[nohn mee pyah-cheh]*	I don't like...
...l'arte	*[.lahr-teh]*	...art
...cucinare	*[coo-chee-nah-reh]*	...cooking
...i film	*[ee feelm]*	...movies
...le discoteche	*[leh dee-skoh-teh-keh]*	...nightclubs
...leggere	*[leh-djeh-reh]*	...reading
...fare shopping/ fare spese	*[fah-reh shopping/ fare speh-zeh]*	...shopping
...lo sport	*[loh sport]*	...sport
...viaggiare	*[viah-djah-reh]*	...traveling
...ballare	*[bahl-lah-reh]*	...to dance
...concerti	*[cohn-chehr-tee]*	... concerts
...musica	*[moo-see-cah]*	...music

Chapter 44: Disabled travelers / Viaggiatori disabili

Listen to track 107

Quali servizi avete per persone disabili?	*[qwah-lee sehr-vee-tsee ah-veh-teh pehr pehr-soh-neh dee-sah-bee-lee]*	What facilities do you have for disabled people?
Ci sono bagni per disabili?	*[chee soh-noh bah-nee pehr dee-sah-bee-lee]*	Are there any toilets for the disabled?
Avete camere da letto al piano terra?	*[ah-veh-teh cah-meh-reh dah leht-toh ahl pyah-noh tehr-rah]*	Do you have any bedrooms on the ground floor?
C'è l'ascensore?	*[cheh lah-shehn-soh-reh]*	Is there a lift?
Dov'è l'ascensore?	*[doh-veh lah-shehn-soh-reh]*	Where is the lift?
Avete sedie a rotelle?	*[ah-veh-teh seh-dee-eh ah roh-tehl-leh]*	Do you have wheelchairs?
Si può visitare ... in sedia a rotelle?	*[see pwoh vee-see-tah-reh ... een seh-dee-ah ah-roh-tehl-leh]*	Can you visit ... in a wheelchair?
Avete un ciclo di induzione?	*[ah-veh-teh oon chee-cloh dee een-doo-tsyoh-neh]*	Do you have an induction loop?

Ci sono sconti per le persone disabili?	*[chee soh-noh scohn-tee pehr leh pehr-soh-neh dee-sah-bee-lee]*	Is there a discount for disabled people?
C'è un posto dove posso sedermi?	*[cheh oon poh-stoh doh-veh pohs-soh seh-dehr-mee]*	Is there somewhere I can sit down?

Chapter 45: With kids / Con i bambini

Listen to track 108

un biglietto per un bambino	*[oon bee-lee-eh-toh pehr oon bahm-bee-noh]*	a child's ticket
Lui/Lei ha ... anni.	*[loo-ee/leh-ee ah ... ahn-nee]*	He/She is ... years old.
C'è uno sconto per i bambini?	*[cheh oo-noh scohn-toh pehr ee bahm-bee-nee]*	Is there a discount for children?
Avete un menu per bambini?	*[ah-veh-teh oon meh-noo pehr bahm-bee-nee]*	Do you have a children's menu?
Si possono portare i bambini?	*[see-pohs-soh-noh pohr-tah-reh ee bahm-bee-nee]*	Is it OK to take children?
Avete...?	*[ah-veh-teh]*	Do you have...?
...seggiolone	*[oon seh-djoh-loh-neh]*	...a high chair
...una culla	*[oo-nah cool-lah]*	...a cot
Ho due figli.	*[hoh doo-eh fee-lee]*	I have two children.
Lei ha figli?	*[leh-ee hah fee-lee]*	Do you have any children?

Part 7: Money, banking, and shopping / Soldi ed acquisti

Whether you like saving money or blowing it before it even reaches your wallet, financial matters are a core part of everyday life. Having the ability to talk about money and a good understanding of monetary terms in Italian will be highly useful when using your Italian in real-life scenarios. If you are traveling in an Italian-speaking country, you will at some point need to ask how much something costs or other such questions related to expenses.

Chapter 46: Money / Soldi

Listen to track 109

sportello bancomat	*[spohr-tehl-loh bahn-coh-maht]*	ATM/cash dispenser
prelievo contanti	*[preh-lee-eh-voh cohn-tahn-tee]*	cash withdrawal
Dove posso cambiare delle banconote?	*[doh-veh pohs-soh cahm-bee-ah-reh dehl-leh bahn-coh-noh-teh]*	Where can I change some money?
Posso pagare in sterline/ euro?	*[pohs-soh pah-gah-reh een stehr-lee-neh/ e-oo-roh]*	Can I pay with pounds/euros?
Posso usare la mia carta in questo bancomat?	*[pohs-soh oo-sah-reh lah mee-ah car-tah een qweh-stoh bahn-coh-maht]*	Can I use my credit card with this ATM/cash dispenser?
Ha da cambiare?	*[hah dah cahm-byah-reh]*	Do you have any change?

Chapter 47: Banking / La banca

Listen to track 110

Dov'è la banca più vicina?	*[doh-veh lah bahn-cah pyoo vee-chee-nah]*	Where is the nearest bank?
Quando apre la banca?	*[qwahn-doh ah-preh lah bahn-cah]*	When does the bank open?
Quando chiude la banca?	*[qwahn-doh kyoo-deh lah bahn-cah]*	When does the bank close?
A quale sportello posso incassare questo?	*[ah qwah-leh spohr-tehl-loh pohs-soh een-cahs-sah-reh qweh-stoh]*	At which window can I cash this?
Può cambiarlo per me?	*[pwoh cahm-bee-ahr-loh pehr meh]*	Can you change this for me?
Incasserai l'assegno?	*[een-cahs-seh-rah-ee lahs-seh-nyoh]*	Will you cash a check?
Non mi dia pezzi troppo grossi.	*[nohn mee dee-ah peh-tsee trohp-poh gross-see]*	Don't give me large bills.
Potrei cambiare?	*[poh-treh-ee cahm-bee-ah-reh]*	May I have some change?

una lettera di credito	*[oo-nah let-teh-rah dee creh-dee-toh]*	a letter of credit
un bonifico bancario	*[oon boh-nee-fee-coh bahn-cah-ree-oh]*	a bank draft
Qual è il tasso di cambio per il dollaro?	*[qwah-leh eel tahs-soh dee cahm-bee oh pehr eel dohl-lah-roh]*	What is the exchange rate on the dollar?
Dov'è...?	*[doh-veh]*	Where's...?
...il bancomat	*[eel bahn-ko-mat]*	...the ATM
...l'ufficio cambi	*[loof-fee-choh cahm-bee]*	...the foreign exchange office

Listen to track 111

Vorrei...	*[vohr-reh-ee]*	I'd like to...
...organizzare un trasferimento	*[ohr-gah-nee-dzah-reh oon trahs-feh-ree-mehn-toh]*	...arrange a transfer
...incassare un assegno	*[een-cahs-sah-reh oon ahs-seh-nyoh]*	...cash a check
...cambiare del denaro	*[cahm-bee-ah-reh dehl deh-nah-roh]*	...change money

...avere un anticipo in contanti	*[ah-veh-reh oon ahn-tee-chee-poh een cohn-tahn-tee]*	...get a cash advance
...prelevare del denaro	*[preh-leh-vah-reh dehl deh-nah-roh]*	...withdraw money
Qual è...?	*[qwah-leh]*	What's...?
...la tariffa per quello	*[lah tah-reef-fah pehr qwehl-loh]*	...the charge for that
...il tasso di cambio	*[eel tahs-soh dee cahm-byoh]*	...the exchange rate
sono ... euro.	*[soh-noh ... eh-oo-roh]*	It's ... euros.
È gratuito.	*[eh grah-too-ee-toh]*	It's free.
È già arrivato il mio denaro?	*[eh djah ahr-ree-vah-toh eel mee-oh deh-nah-roh]*	Has my money arrived yet?

Chapter 48: Paying / I pagamenti

Listen to track 112

il conto	*[eel cohn-toh]*	the bill (restaurant)
la ricevuta	*[lah ree-cheh-voo-tah]*	the bill (hotel)
la fattura	*[lah faht-tooh-rah]*	the invoice
la cassa	*[lah cahs-sah]*	the desk
Quanto costa?	*[qwahn-toh coh-stah]*	How much is it?
Quanto costerà?	*[qwahn-toh coh-steh-rah]*	How much will it be?
Posso pagare...?	*[pohs-soh pah-gah-reh]*	Can I pay...?
...con carta di credito	*[.cohn cahr-tah dee creh-dee-toh]*	...by credit card
...con assegno	*[cohn ahs-seh-nyoh]*	...by check
Lo metta sul mio conto.	*[loh meht-tah sool mee-oh cohn-toh]*	Put it on my bill. (at the hotel)
Dove pago?	*[doh-veh pah-goh]*	Where do I pay?
Accettate carte di credito?	*[ah-tchet-tah-teh cahr-teh dee creh-dee-toh]*	Do you take credit cards?

Il servizio è incluso?	*[eel sehr-vee-tsyoh eh een-cloo-soh]*	Is service included?
Può darmi lo scontrino, per favore?	*[pwoh dahr-mee loh scohn-tree-noh, pehr fah-voh-reh]*	Could you give me a receipt, please?
Pago in anticipo?	*[pah-goh een ahn-tee-chee-poh]*	Do I pay in advance?
Non ho soldi spiccioli	*[nohn hoh sohl-dee spee-tcho-lee]*	I have nothing smaller/no small change.

Chapter 49: Luggage / I bagagli

Listen to track 113

ritiro bagagli	*[ree-tee-roh bah-gah-lee]*	baggage reclaim
deposito bagagli	*[deh-poh-see-toh bah-gah-lee]*	left luggage
trolley	*[troll-leh-ee]*	luggage trolley
Il mio bagaglio non è ancora arrivato.	*[eel mee-oh bah-gah-lee-oh nohn eh ahn-coh-rah ahr-ree-vah-toh]*	My luggage hasn't arrived yet.
la mia valigia è stata danneggiata in volo.	*[lah mee-ah vah-lee-djah eh stah-tah dahn-neh-djah-tah een voh-loh]*	My suitcase has been damaged in flight.

Chapter 50: Repairs / Riparazioni

Listen to track 114

calzolaio	*[cahl-tsoh-lah-yoh]*	shoe repairer
È rotto.	*[eh roht-toh]*	This is broken.
Dove posso farlo riparare?	*[doh-veh pohs-soh fahr-loh ree-pah-rah-reh]*	Where can I get this repaired?
Può aggiustare...?	*[pwoh ah-djoo-stah-reh]*	Can you repair...?
...queste scarpe	*[qweh-steh scahr-peh]*	...these shoes
...il mio orologio	*[eel mee-oh oh-roh-loh-djoh]*	...my watch
...i miei occhiali	*[ee mee-eh-ee oh-kee-ah-lee]*	...my glasses
Quanto tempo occorre?	*[qwan-toh tehm-poh oh-cohr-reh]*	How long will it take?
Potrebbe riparare il mio ...?	*[poh-trehb-beh ree-pah-rah-reh eel mee-oh]*	Can I have my ... repaired?
È difettoso.	*[eh dee-feht-toh-soh]*	It's faulty.

Chapter 51: Laundry / In lavanderia

Listen to track 115

tintoria	_[teen-toh-ree-ah]_	dry cleaner's
lavanderia/ lavanderia a gettoni	_[lah-vahn-deh-ree-ah/ lah-vahn-deh-ree-ah ah djet-toh-nee]_	launderette/ laundromat
detersivo in polvere	_[deh-tehr-see-voh een pohl-veh-reh]_	washing powder (laundry soap)
stirare	_[stee-rah-reh]_	ironing

Chapter 52: Shopping / Acquisti

Listen to track 116

Voglio fare shopping.	_[voh-lyoh fah-reh shopping]_	I want to go shopping.
Mi piace quello.	_[mee pyah-tcheh qwehl-loh]_	I like that.
Quanto costa?	_[qwahn-toh coh-stah]_	How much is it?
È molto costoso.	_[eh mohl-toh coh-stoh-soh]_	It is very expensive.
Preferisco qualcosa di migliore/più economico.	_[preh-feh-rees-coh qwal-coh-sah dee mee-lyoh-reh/pyoo eh-coh-noh-mee-coh]_	I prefer something better/ cheaper.
Ne avete altri?	_[neh ah-veh-teh ahl-tree]_	Do you have any others?
Può mostrarmene altri?	_[pwoh moh-strahr-meh-neh ahl-tree]_	Could you show me some others?
Posso provarlo?	_[pohs-soh proh-vahr-loh]_	May I try this on?
Posso ordinarne uno?	_[pohs-soh ohr-dee-nahr-neh oo-noh]_	Can I order one?
Per favore prenda le mie misure.	_[pehr fah-voh reh prehn-dah leh mee-eh mee-soo-reh]_	Please take my measurements.

135

Può spedirlo a New York?	[pwoh speh-deer-loh ah New York]	Can you ship it to New York City?
Può spedirlo all'estero?	[pwoh speh-deer-loh ahl-leh-steh-roh]	Can I have it sent overseas?
A chi pago?	[ah kee pah-goh]	Whom do I pay?
Mi invii il conto.	[mee een-vee eel cohn-toh]	Please bill me.

Listen to track 117

Voglio comprare una cuffia da bagno.	[voh-lee-oh cohm-prah-reh oo-nah coof-fyah dah bah-nyoh]	I want to buy a bathing cap.
...un costume da bagno	[oon coh-stoo-meh dah bah-nyoh]	...a bathing suit
...un reggiseno	[oon reh-djee-seh-noh]	...a brassiere
...un abito	[oon ah-bee-toh]	...a dress
...un abito	[oon ah-bee-toh]	...a suit
...una camicetta	[oo-nah cah-mee-chet-tah]	...a blouse
...un cappotto	[oon cah-pot-toh]	...a coat

...un paio di guanti	*[oon pah-yoh dee gwahn-tee]*	...a pair of gloves
...una borsa	*[oo-nah bohr-sah]*	...a handbag
...dei fazzoletti	*[deh-ee fah-tsoh-leht-tee]*	...some handkerchiefs
...un cappello	*[oon cahp-pehl-loh]*	...a hat
...una giacca	*[oo-nah djak-cah]*	...a jacket
...della biancheria intima	*[dehl-lah bee-ahn-keh-ree-ah een-tee-mah]*	...some lingerie
...della biancheria intima	*[dehl-lah bee-ahn-keh-ree-ah een-tee-mah]*	...some underwear
...una camicia da notte	*[oo-nah cah-mee-tcha dah noht-teh]*	... a nightgown
...un impermeabile	*[oon eem-pehr-meh-ah-bee-leh]*	...a raincoat
...un paio di scarpe	*[oon pah-yoh dee scahr-peh]*	...a pair of shoes
...dei lacci	*[deh-ee lah-tchee]*	...some shoelaces
...un paio di pantofole	*[oon pah-yoh dee pahn-toh-foh-leh]*	...a pair of slippers

...un paio di calze	*[oon pah-yoh dee cahl-tseh]*	...a pair of socks
...un paio di collant	*[oon pah-yoh dee cohl-lahnt]*	...a pair of nylon
...un maglione	*[oon mah-lyoh-neh]*	...a sweater
...delle cravatte	*[dehl-leh crah-vaht-teh]*	...some ties
...pantaloni	*[pahn-tah-loh-nee]*	...trousers

Listen to track 118

Avete dei posacenere?	*[ah-veh-teh deh-ee poh-sah-cheh-neh-reh]*	Do you have some ashtrays?
...una scatola di dolci	*[oo-nah scah-toh-lah dee dohl-chee]*	...a box of candy
...della porcellana	*[dehl-lah pohr-tchel-lah-nah]*	...some porcelain
...delle bambole	*[dehl-leh bahm-boh-leh]*	...some dolls
...degli orecchini	*[deh-lee oh-reh-kee-nee]*	...some earrings
...del profumo	*[dehl proh-foo-moh]*	...some perfume

...dei quadri	*[deh-ee qwah-dree]*	...some pictures
...dei dischi	*[deh-ee dees-kee]*	...some records
...dell' argenteria	*[dehl-lahr-djen-teh-ree-ah]*	...some silverware
...dei giocattoli	*[deh-ee djoh-caht-toh-lee]*	...some toys
...un ombrello	*[oon ohm-brehl-loh]*	...an umbrella
...un orologio	*[oon oh-roh-loh-djoh]*	...a watch
...una cinta	*[oo-nah cheen-tah]*	...a belt

Listen to track 119

Dov'è...?	*[doh-veh]*	Where's...?
...la libreria	*[lah lee-breh-ree-ah]*	...the bookshop
...il grande magazzino/	*[eel grahn-deh mah-gah-dzee-noh]*	... the department store
...il supermercato	*[eel soo-pehr-mehr-cah-toh]*	...the grocery store
...il supermercato	*[eel soo-pehr-mehr-cah-toh]*	...the supermarket
Dove posso comprare (un lucchetto)?	*[doh-veh pohs-soh cohm-prah-reh (oon look-keh-toh)]*	Where can I buy (a padlock)?

139

Sto cercando...	*[stoh cher-cahn-doh]*	I'm looking for...
Posso vederlo?	*[pohs-soh veh-dehr-loh]*	Can I look at it?
Ha la garanzia?	*[ah lah gah-rahn-tsee-ah]*	Does it have a guarantee?

Listen to track 120

Per favore, vorrei...	*[pehr fah-voh-reh, voh-reh-ee]*	I'd like ..., please.
una busta	*[oo-nah boo-stah]*	a bag
un rimborso	*[oon reem-bohr-soh]*	a refund
restituire questo	*[reh-stee-too-ee-reh qweh-stoh]*	to return this
Potrebbe scrivere il prezzo?	*[poh-treh-beh scree-veh-reh eel preh-tsoh]*	Can you write down the price?
Può ridurre il prezzo?	*[pwoh ree-doo-reh eel preh-tsoh]*	Can you lower the price?
Le darò (cinque) euro.	*[leh dah-roh (cheen-qweh) eh-oo-roh]*	I'll give you (five) euros.
C'è un errore nel conto.	*[cheh oon eh-roh-reh nehl cohn-toh]*	There's a mistake in the bill.

Chapter 53: Making complaints / Fare reclami

Non funziona.	*[nohn foon-tsee-oh-nah]*	This doesn't work.
È sporco.	*[eh spohr-coh]*	It's dirty.
la luce	*[lah loo-cheh]*	light
la serratura	*[lah sehr-rah-too-rah]*	lock
il riscaldamento	*[eel rees-cahl-dah-mehn-toh]*	heating
l'aria condizionata	*[lah-ree-ah con-dee-tsyoh-nah-tah]*	air conditioning
È rotto.	*[eh rott-toh]*	It's broken.
Voglio un rimborso.	*[voh-lee-oh oon reem-bohr-soh]*	I want a refund.

Chapter 54: Problems / Problematiche

Può aiutarmi?	*[pwoh ah-yoo-tahr-mee]*	Can you help me?
Parlo poco italiano.	*[pahr-loh poh-coh ee-tah-lyah-noh]*	I speak very little Italian.
Qualcuno qui parla Inglese?	*[qwahl-coo-noh qwee pahr-lah ee.n-gleh-seh]*	Does anyone here speak English?
Vorrei parlare con il responsabile.	*[voh-reh-ee pahr-lah-reh cohn eel reh-spohn-sah-bee-leh]*	I would like to speak to whoever is in charge.
Mi sono perso.	*[mee soh-noh pehr-soh]*	I'm lost.
Come arrivo a...?	*[coh-meh ah-ree-voh ah]*	How do I get to...?
Ho perso...	*[oh pehr-soh]*	I missed...
...il mio treno	*[eel myoh treh-noh]*	...my train
...il mio volo	*[eel myoh voh-loh]*	...my plane
...la mia coincidenza	*[lah mee-ah coh-een-chee-dehn-tsah]*	...my connection

Ho perso il mio volo perché c'era uno sciopero	*[oh pehr-soh eel myoh voh-loh pehr-keh che-rah oo-noh shoh-peh-roh]*	I've missed my flight because there was a strike
Può mostrarmi come funziona?	*[pwoh moss-trahr-mee coh-meh foon-tsyoh-nah]*	Can you show me how this works?
Ho perso il mio portafoglio.	*[hoh pehr-soh eel myoh pohr-tah-foh-lyoh]*	I have lost my purse.
Ho bisogno di andare a...	*[hoh bee-soh-nyoh dee ahn-dah-reh ah]*	I need to get to...
Lasciatemi solo!	*[lah-shah-teh-mee soh-loh]*	Leave me alone!
Andate via!	*[ahn-dah-teh vee-ah]*	Go away!

Chapter 55: Emergencies / Emergenze

Listen to track 123

La prego, chiami...	*[lah preh-goh, kyah-mee]*	Please call...
...la polizia	*[lah poh-lee-tsee-ah]*	...the police
...un' ambulanza	*[oon ahm-boo-lahn-tsah]*	...an ambulance
...i vigili del fuoco	*[ee vee-djee-lee dehl fwoh-coh]*	...the fire brigade (fire department)
...la stazione di polizia	*[lah stah-tsee-oh neh dee poh-lee-tsee-ah]*	...police station
Dov'è la stazione di polizia?	*[doh-veh lah stah-tsee-oh neh dee poh-lee-tsee-ah]*	Where is the police station?
pronto soccorso	*[prohn-toh soh-cohr-soh]*	accident and emergency department
Aiuto!	*[ah-yoo-toh]*	Help!
Al fuoco!	*[ahl fwoh-coh]*	Fire!
Può aiutarmi?	*[pwoh ah-yoo-tahr-mee]*	Can you help me?
C'è stato un incidente.	*[cheh stah-toh oon een-chee-dehn-teh]*	There has been an accident.

Qualcuno è stato ferito.	*[qwal-coo-noh eh stah-toh feh-ree-toh]*	Someone has been injured.
Vorrei denunciare un furto.	*[voh-reh-ee deh-noon-chah-reh oon foor-toh]*	I want to report a theft.
Sono stato derubato/ attaccato.	*[soh-noh stah-toh deh-roo-bah-toh/ah-tah-kah-toh]*	I've been robbed/ attacked.
Sono stata stuprata.	*[soh-noh stah-tah stoo-prah-tah]*	I've been raped.

Listen to track 124

Voglio parlare con un'agente di polizia donna.	*[voh-lyoh pahr-lah-reh cohn uhn ah-djehn-teh dee poh-lee-tsee-ah dohn-nah]*	I want to speak to a policewoman.
hanno rubato...	*[hah-noh roo-bah-toh]*	Someone has stolen...
...la mia borsa	*[lah mee-ah bohr-sah]*	...my handbag
...i miei soldi	*[ee mee-eh-ee sohl-dee]*	...my money
La mia auto è stata scassinata.	*[lah mee-ah ah-oo-toh eh stah-tah skah-see-nah-tah]*	My car has been broken into.
La mia auto è stata rubata.	*[lah mee-ah ah-oo-toh eh stah-tah roo-bah-tah]*	My car has been stolen.

Ho bisogno di fare una telefonata.	*[hoh bee-soh-nyoh dee fah-reh oo-nah teh-leh-foh-nah-tah]*	I need to make a telephone call.
Mi serve un verbale per la mia assicurazione.	*[mee sehr-veh oon vehr-bah-leh pehr la mee-ah ah-see-coo-rah-tsyoh-neh]*	I need a report for my insurance.
Non conoscevo il limite di velocità.	*[non coh-noh-sheh-voh eel lee-mee-teh dee veh-loh-chee-tah]*	I didn't know the speed limit.
Quant'è la multa?	*[qwahn-teh lah mool-tah]*	How much is the fine?
Dove posso pagarla?	*[doh-veh poh-soh pah-gahr-lah]*	Where do I pay it?
Devo pagarla subito?	*[deh-voh pah-gahr-lah soo-bee-toh]*	Do I have to pay it straight away?
Mi dispiace, agente.	*[mee dees-pyah-cheh, ah-jen-teh]*	I'm very sorry, officer.
Lei è passato con il rosso.	*[leh-ee eh pahs-sah-toh cohn eel rohs-soh]*	You went through a red light.
Lei non ha dato la precedenza.	*[leh-ee non hah dah-toh lah preh-tcheh-dehn-tsah]*	You didn't give way.

Part 8: Health and illness / La salute e le malattie

If you are traveling to an Italian-speaking country, you will need to know some health-related vocabulary. Whether you require pain-killers from the pharmacy or have an emergency doctor's visit while abroad, you will likely encounter health-related situations and it is an invaluable skill to be able to speak the necessary Italian to navigate such issues.

Chapter 56: At the pharmacy / La farmacia

Listen to track 125

la farmacia	*[la fahr-mah-chee-ah]*	pharmacy
la farmacia di turno	*[la fahr-mah-chee-ah dee toor-noh]*	duty chemist's
Può darmi qualcosa per...?	*[pwoh dahr-mee qwahl-coh-sah pehr]*	Can you give me something for...?
...il mal di testa	*[eel mahl dee teh-stah]*	...a headache
...il mal d'auto	*[eel mahl dah-oo-toh]*	...car sickness
...l'influenza	*[leen-floo-ehn-tsah]*	...the flu
...la diarrea	*[lah dee-ah-reh-ah]*	...diarrhea
...le scottature	*[leh scott-tah-too-reh]*	...sunburn
È adatto per bambini?	*[eh ah-dah-toh pehr ee bahm-bee-nee]*	Is it safe for children?
Quanto devo dargliene?	*[qwahn-toh deh-voh dahr-lee-eh-neh]*	How much should I give him/her?

Chapter 57: Dealing with medical issues / Problemi di salute

Listen to track 126

un dentista	*[oon dehn-tees-tah]*	a dentist
un dottore	*[oon doh-toh-reh]*	a doctor
un ospedale	*[oon oh-speh-dah-leh]*	a hospital
una farmacia (notturna)	*[oo-nah fahr-mah-chee-ah (noh-toor-nah)]*	a (night) pharmacist
Ho bisogno di un medico (che parli inglese).	*[hoh bee-soh-nyoh dee oon doc-toh-reh (keh pahr-lee een-gleh-seh)]*	I need a doctor (who speaks English).
Potrei vedere una dottoressa?	*[poh-treh-ee veh-deh-reh oo-nah doh-toh-reh-sah]*	Could I see a female doctor?
Ho finito le mie medicine.	*[hoh fee-nee-toh leh mee-eh meh-dee-chee-neh]*	I've run out of my medication.
Sono malato.	*[soh-noh mah-lah-toh]*	I'm sick.
Mi fa male qui.	*[mee fah mah-leh qwee]*	It hurts here.

Listen to track 127

Io ho...	[ee-oh hoh]	I have (a)...
...l'asma	[lahs-mah]	...asthma
...la bronchite	[lah brohn-kee-teh]	...bronchitis
...la stipsi	[lah steep-seeh]	...constipation
...la tosse	[lah tohs-seh]	...cough
...la diarrea	[lah dee-ah-reh-ah]	...diarrhea
...la febbre	[lah feh-breh]	...fever
...il mal di testa	[eel mahl dee teh-stah]	...headache
...problemi di cuore	[proh-bleh-mee dee qwoh-reh]	...heart condition
...la nausea	[lah nah-oo-seh-ah]	...nausea
...dolore	[doh-loh-reh]	...pain
...la gola infiammata	[lah goh-lah een-fee-ah-mah-tah]	...sore throat
...mal di denti	[mahl dee dehn-tee]	...toothache

Listen to track 128

Sono allergico...	[soh-noh ahl-lehr-djee-coh]	I'm allergic to...

...agli antibiotici	*[ahl-lee ahn-tee-byoh-tee-chee]*	...antibiotics
...agli anti-nfiammatori	*[ah-lee ahn-tee-een-fee-ahm-mah-toh-ree]*	...anti-inflammatories
...agli antidolorifici	*[ah-lee ahn-tee-doh-loh-ree-fee-chee]*	...painkillers
...all'aspirina	*[ah-lah-spee-ree-nah]*	...aspirin
...alle api	*[ah-leh ah-pee]*	...bees
...alla codeina	*[ahl-lah coh-deh-ee-nah]*	...codeine
...alla penicellina	*[ahl-lah peh-nee-chell-lee-nah]*	...penicillin
...all' antisettico	*[ahl-lahn-tee-sett-tee-coh]*	...antiseptic
...bende	*[behn-deh]*	...bandage
...preservativi	*[preh-sehr-vah-tee-vee]*	...condoms
...contra-ccettivi	*[cohn-trah-tchet-tee-vee]*	...contraceptives
...repellente per insetti	*[reh-pehl-lehn-teh pehr een-seht-teeh]*	...insect repellent
...lassativi	*[lah-tsah-tee-vee]*	...laxatives

...sali di reidratazione	*[sah-lee dee reh-eee-drah-tah-tsyoh-neh]*	...rehydration salts
...sonniferi	*[sohn-nee-feh-ree]*	...sleeping tablets

Listen to track 129

Vorrei vedere un dottore americano.	*[vohr-reh-ee veh-deh-reh oon doh-toh-reh ah-meh-ree-cah-noh]*	I wish to see an American doctor.
Non dormo bene.	*[nohn dohr-moh beh-neh]*	I do not sleep well.
Mi fa male la testa.	*[mee fah mah-leh lah teh-stah]*	My head aches.
Devo restare a letto?	*[deh-voh reh-stah-reh ah leht-toh]*	Must I stay in bed?
Posso alzarmi?	*[pohs-soh ahl-zahr-mee]*	May I get up?
Mi sento meglio.	*[mee sehn-toh meh-lee-oh]*	I feel better.

Chapter 58: Seeing a doctor / Dal dottore

Listen to track 130

ospedale	[oh-speh-dah-leh]	hospital
pronto soccorso	[prohn-toh soh-cohr-soh]	accident and emergency department
consultazioni	[cohn-sool-tah-tsyoh-nee]	consultations
Mi sento male.	[mee sehn-toh mah-leh]	I feel ill.
Ha la febbre?	[hah lah feh-breh]	Do you have a temperature?
No, mi fa male qui.	[noh, mee fah mah-leh qwee]	No, I have a pain here.
Mi serve un medico.	[mee sehr-veh oon meh-dee-coh]	I need a doctor.
Mio figlio/ Mia figlia è malato/a.	[mee-oh fee-lyoh/mee-ah fee-lyah eh mah-lah-toh/ mah-lah-tah]	My son/My daughter is ill.
Sono diabetico.	[soh-noh dee-ah-beh-tee-coh]	I'm diabetic.
Sono incinta.	[soh-noh een-cheen-tah]	I'm pregnant.
Prendo la pillola.	[prehn-doh lah peel-loh-lah]	I'm on the pill.

Mi serve la ricevuta per l'assicurazione.	*[mee sehr-veh lah ree-cheh-voo-tah pehr lah-see-coo-rah-tsyoh-neh]*	I need a receipt for the insurance.

Chapter 59: Seeing a dentist / Dal dentista

Listen to track 131

Ho bisogno di un dentista.	_[hoh bee-soh-nyoh dee oon dehn-tee-stah]_	I need to see a dentist.
Ha mal di denti.	_[hah mahl dee dehn-tee]_	He/She has toothache.
Può fare un'otturazione temporanea?	_[pwoh fah-reh oon ott-too-rah-tsyoh-neh tehm-poh-rah-neh-ah]_	Can you do a temporary filling?
Può darmi qualcosa per il dolore?	_[pwoh dahr-mee qwahl-coh-sah pehr eel doh-loh-reh]_	Can you give me something for the pain?
Fa male.	_[fah mah-leh]_	It hurts.
Può riparare la mia dentiera?	_[pwoh ree-pah-rah-reh lah mee-ah dehn-tee-eh-rah]_	Can you repair my dentures?
Devo pagare?	_[deh-voh pah-gah-reh]_	Do I have to pay?
Quanto costerà?	_[qwahn-toh coh-steh-rah]_	How much will it be?
Mi serve la ricevuta per l'assicurazione.	_[mee sehr-veh lah ree-cheh-voo-tah pehr lah-see-coo-rah-tsyoh-neh]_	I need a receipt for the insurance.

Part 9: Miscellaneous / Varie

If you want more additional phrases. ☺

Chapter 60: Liquid / I liquidi

Listen to track 132

mezzo litro di...	*[med-zoh lee-troh dee]*	1/2 liter of...
un litro di...	*[oon lee-troh dee]*	a liter of...
mezza bottiglia di...	*[med-zah boh-tee-lyah dee]*	1/2 bottle of...
una bottiglia di...	*[oo-nah boh-tee-lyah dee]*	a bottle of...
un bicchiere di...	*[oon bee-kee-eh-reh dee]*	a glass of...

Chapter 61: Quantity / Quantità

Listen to track 133

100 grammi di/ un etto di...	*[chen-toh grahm-mee dee/oon eht-toh dee]*	100 grams of ...
mezzo chilo di...	*[med-zoh kee-loh dee]*	a half kilo of...
un kilo di...	*[oon kee-loh dee]*	a kilo of...
una fetta di...	*[oo-nah feht-tah dee]*	a slice of ...
una porzione di...	*[oo-nah pohr-tsyoh-neh dee]*	a portion of ...
una dozzina	*[oo-nah doh-zee-nah]*	a dozen
una scatola di...	*[oo-nah scah-toh-lah dee]*	a box of ...
un pacchetto di...	*[oon pah-ket-toh dee]*	a packet of ...

Listen to track 134

un cartone di...	*[oon cahr-toh-neh dee]*	a carton of...
un barattolo di...	*[oon bah-raht-toh-loh dee]*	a jar of...
500 euro di...	*[cheen-qweh-chen-toh e-oo-roh dee]*	500 euros of...
un quarto	*[oon qwahr-toh]*	a quarter

dieci per cento	*[dee-eh-chee pehr chen-toh]*	ten per cent
più...	*[pyoo]*	more ...
meno...	*[meh-noh]*	less...
abbastanza di...	*[ah-bah-stahn-tsah dee]*	enough of...
il doppio	*[eel dohp-pyoh]*	double
due volte	*[doo-eh vohl-teh]*	twice
una volta	*[oo-nah vohl-tah]*	once

Chapter 62: Cardinal numbers / I numeri cardinali

Listen to track 135

zero	*[zeh-roh]*	0
uno	*[oo-noh]*	1
due	*[doo-eh]*	2
tre	*[treh]*	3
quattro	*[qwah-troh]*	4
cinque	*[cheen-qweh]*	5
sei	*[seh-ee]*	6
sette	*[seht-teh]*	7
otto	*[oht-toh]*	8
nove	*[noh-veh]*	9
dieci	*[dee-eh-chee]*	10
undici	*[oon-dee-chee]*	11
dodici	*[doh-dee-chee]*	12
tredici	*[treh-dee-chee]*	13
quattordici	*[qwah-tohr-dee-chee]*	14
quindici	*[qween-dee-chee]*	15
sedici	*[seh-dee-chee]*	16
diciassette	*[dee-chah-seht-teh]*	17
diciotto	*[dee-chot-toh]*	18
diciannove	*[dee-chan-noh-veh]*	19
venti	*[vehn-tee]*	20

Listen to track 136

ventuno	[vehn-too-noh]	21
ventidue	[vehn-tee-doo-eh]	22
ventitré	[vehn-tee-treh]	23
trenta	[trehn-tah]	30
trentuno	[trehn-too-noh]	31
trentadue	[trehn-tah-doo-eh]	32
quaranta	[qwah-rahn-tah]	40
quarantuno	[qwah-rahn-too-noh]	41
quarantadue	[qwah-rahn-tah-doo-eh]	42
cinquanta	[cheen-qwahn-tah]	50
sessanta	[seh-sahn-tah]	60
settanta	[seht-tahn-tah]	70
ottanta	[ott-tahn-tah]	80
novanta	[noh-vahn-tah]	90
cento	[chen-toh]	100
centodieci	[chen-toh-dee-eh-chee]	110
duecento	[doo-eh-chen-toh]	200
duecento-cinquanta	[doo-eh-chen-toh-cheen-qwahn-tah]	250
mille	[meel-leh]	1,000
un milione	[oon mee-lyoh-neh]	one million

Chapter 63: What time is it? / Che ora è?

Listen to track 137

Che ora è?	*[keh oh-rah eh]*	What time is it?
È l'una.	*[eh loo-nah]*	It's one o'clock.
È mezzanotte.	*[eh meh-dzah-not-teh]*	It's midnight.
Sono...	*[soh-noh]*	It's ...
...le due	*[eh doo-eh]*	...two o'clock
...le tre	*[leh treh]*	...three o'clock
...le nove e dieci	*[leh noh-veh eh dee-eh-chee]*	...9:10
...le nove e un quarto	*[leh noh-veh eh oon qwahr-toh]*	...quarter past 9
...le nove e mezza	*[leh noh-veh eh meh-tsah]*	...9:30
...le nove e trentacinque	*[leh noh-veh eh trehn-tah-cheen-qweh]*	...9:35
...le dieci meno un quarto	*[eh dee-eh-chee meh-noh oon qwahr-toh]*	...quarter to 10
...le dieci meno dieci	*[...leh dee-eh-chee meh-noh dee-eh-chee]*	...10 to 10

162

A che ora...?	*[ah keh oh-rah]*	When does i ...?
... apre/ chiude/ inizia/finisce	*[... ah-preh/ kyoo-deh/ee-nee-tsyah/ fee-nee-sheh]*	... open/close/ begin/finish
alle tre	*[ahl-leh treh]*	at three o'clock
prima delle tre	*[pree-mah dehl-leh treh]*	before three o'clock
dopo le tre	*[doh-poh leh treh]*	after three o'clock

Listen to track 138

oggi	*[oh-djee]*	today
stasera	*[stah-seh-rah]*	tonight
domani	*[doh-mah-nee]*	tomorrow
ieri	*[yeh-ree]*	yesterday
avant'ieri	*[ah-vahn-tee-yeh-ree]*	the day before yesterday
la scorsa notte	*[lah scohr-sah nott-teh]*	last night
dopodomani	*[doh-poh-doh-mah-nee]*	the day after tomorrow
la mattina/il mattino	*[lah mah-tee-nah/eel mah-tee-noh]*	the morning
il pomeriggio	*[eel poh-meh-ree-djoh]*	the afternoon
la sera	*[lah seh-rah]*	the evening
la notte	*[lah nott-teh]*	the night

la prossima settimana	*[lah pross-see-mah seht-tee-mah-nah]*	next week
la scorsa settimana	*[lah scohr-sah seht-tee-mah-nah]*	last week
questo mese	*[qweh-stoh meh-seh]*	this month

Chapter 64: Days of the week / I giorni della *settimana*

Listen to track 139

Lunedì	*[loo-neh-dee]*	Monday
Martedì	*[mar-teh-dee]*	Tuesday
Mercoledì	*[mehr-coh-leh-dee]*	Wednesday
Giovedì	*[djoh-veh-dee]*	Thursday
Venerdì	*[veh-nehr-dee]*	Friday
Sabato	*[sah-bah-toh]*	Saturday
Domenica	*[doh-meh-nee-cah]*	Sunday

Chapter 65: Months of the year / I mesi dell'anno

Listen to track 140

Gennaio	*[jen-nah-yoh]*	January
Febbraio	*[feb-brah-yoh]*	February
Marzo	*[mar-tsoh]*	March
Aprile	*[ah-pree-leh]*	April
Maggio	*[mah-djoh]*	May
Giugno	*[joo-nyoh]*	June
Luglio	*[loo-lyoh]*	July
Agosto	*[ah-goh-stoh]*	August
Settembre	*[set-tehm-breh]*	September
Ottobre	*[ott-toh-breh]*	October
Novembre	*[noh-vehm-breh]*	November
Dicembre	*[dee-chem-breh]*	December

Chapter 66: Types of season / Le stagioni

Listen to track 141

primavera	*[pree-mah-veh-rah]*	spring
estate	*[eh-stah-teh]*	summer
autunno	*[ah-oo-toon-noh]*	autumn
inverno	*[een-vehr-noh]*	winter

Chapter 67: Colors & shapes / Colori e forme

Listen to track 142

verde	*[vehr-deh]*	green
blu	*[bloo]*	blue
celeste	*[cheh-leh-steh]*	light blue
rosso	*[rohs-soh]*	red
nero	*[neh-roh]*	black
rosa	*[roh-sah]*	pink
bianco	*[byahn-coh]*	white
arancione	*[ah-rahn-choh-neh]*	orange
giallo	*[djah-loh]*	yellow
grigio	*[gree-djoh]*	grey
viola	*[vyoh-lah]*	purple
marrone	*[mah-roh-neh]*	brown
cerchio	*[cher-kyoh]*	circle
quadrato	*[qwah-drah-toh]*	square
rettangolo	*[rett-tahn-goh-loh]*	rectangle
rombo	*[rom-boh]*	rhombus
triangolo	*[tree-ahn-goh-loh]*	triangle
cubo	*[coo-boh]*	cube

Chapter 68: Measurements / Misure

Listen to track 143

Qual è la lunghezza?	*[qwah-leh lah loon-gweh-tsah]*	What is the length?
la larghezza	*[lah lahr-gweh-tsah]*	the width
la taglia	*[lah tah-lyah]*	the size
altezza	*[ahl-teh-tsah]*	height
Quant'è al metro?	*[qwahn-teh ahl meh-troh]*	How much is it per meter?
È 10 metri di lunghezza per 4 di larghezza.	*[eh dee-eh-chee meh-tree dee loon-gweh-tsah pehr qwah-troh dee lahr-gweh-tsah]*	It is ten meters long by four meters wide.
alto	*[ahl-toh]*	high
basso	*[bahs-soh]*	low
largo	*[lahr-goh]*	large
piccolo	*[peek-koh-loh]*	small
medio	*[meh-dyoh]*	medium
simile	*[see-mee-leh]*	alike
diverso	*[dee-vehr-soh]*	different
un paio	*[oon pah-yoh]*	a pair
una dozzina	*[oo-nah doh-tsee-nah]*	a dozen
una mezza dozzina	*[oo-nah meh-dzah doh-tsee-nah]*	a half dozen

Conclusion

Italian is an incredibly beautiful language to learn. Whether you're learning these phrases as a way to boost your Italian language studies or to help you enjoy your Italian holiday, we hope this book was able to help you achieve your goals.

If you have a few minutes to spare, please let us know your thoughts about this book by sending an email to contact@talkinitalian.com. We'd be delighted to receive any feedback from you. Any suggestions on how we could further improve this book will be very much welcome. My team and I are always looking for ways to improve our products so that they can be of greater help to language learners like you.

For more insights about the Italian language and culture, do visit our website at Talkinitalian.com. We are always working towards providing useful content for you.

And so with that, we say our goodbyes.

Grazie.

The Talk in Italian Team

How to download the Audio

Please take note that the audio files are in MP3 format and need to be accessed online. No worries though; it's quite easy!

On your computer, smartphone, iphone/ipad, or tablet, simply go to this link:

https://talkinitalian.com/phrasebook-audio/

If you have any problems downloading the audio, feel free to send an email to support@talkinitalian.com. We'll do our best to assist you, but we would greatly appreciate it if you could thoroughly review the instructions first.

Grazie,

The Talk in Italian Team

I am here to help

I love my language and culture and would love to share it with you.

Should you have any questions regarding my book, the Italian language and culture, or technical issues, I am happy to answer them. You can contact me via email at support@ talkinitalian.com

Printed in Great Britain
by Amazon

81653063R00108